Explore Australia's NORTHERN TERRITORY

Introduced by LES HIDDINS, 'THE BUSH TUCKER MAN'

Written by
FRANK ALCORTA

The Northern Territory is like no other place on earth. It is the living remnants of Gondwanaland, the chunk of the earth's crust that broke away from its mother continent in Africa and drifted away to develop in ways that not even nature ever thought possible.

This book is primarily a book about discovery. It is about a journey that will take you to sights and scenery that do not exist anywhere else.

NATIONAL
BOOK DISTRIBUTORS
AND PUBLISHERS

Published by
National Book Distributors and Publishers
Unit 3, 2 Aquatic Drive, Frenchs Forest, NSW 2086
Devised and produced by Conservation Commission of the Northern Territory
Text by Frank Alcorta
Original layout and design by Presentations Pty Ltd, Darwin
Additional layout (Second Revised Edition) by Veronica Hilton
Cover design by National Book Distributors and Publishers
Publishing Consultant: Stephen Davis
Typesetting processed by North Type Pty Ltd, Darwin
Printed by Kyodo Printing Co. (S'pore) Pte Ltd
First Edition 1989
Revised Edition 1992 (Limp)
Second Revised Edition 1994, Reprinted 1995
© Conservation Commission of the Northern Territory 1989

National Library of Australia
Cataloguing-in-Publication data

Alcorta, Frank
Explore Australia's Northern Territory.

2nd ed.
Includes index.
ISBN 1 875580 36 0

1. Northern Territory—Description and travel—1975-1990.
1. Title.

919.4290463

CONTENTS

A MESSAGE FROM LES HIDDINS
'THE BUSH TUCKER MAN'

My involvement with the Northern Territory goes back quite a long way. For years and years I had been coming through here, camping under the occasional gum tree, just doing my job. Then, about five or six years ago, I bumped into an old mate of mine, a bloke called Frank Alcorta. The truth of the matter is that Frank was my original Platoon Sergeant in Vietnam, way back in the days when I was a private soldier.

Anyway, to cut a long story short, Frank has written the text for this book and neither of us would have guessed, twenty-odd years ago in Vietnam, that things would one day come to this. But then again, the Territory has a mystique and a magic about it that sometimes works in pretty strange ways. It is something that you have to experience to fully appreciate.

I can't think of any other way to describe the Territory but as a land with a difference, perhaps the world's last great unknown. In all my years of roaming around the deserts and plains of Central Australia, the forest country, the ranges, wetlands and rivers of the Top End, and the great empty land in the middle, I have always been struck by one thought—that out here, nature is the boss.

Roads and towns have been built, mines cut out and settlements established. Electricity lines sometimes break the bare landscape and, on remote hilltops, telecommunication towers remind you that this is an age of technology.

But the overwhelming feeling I always have is that this is a wild, untamed land, basically untouched by civilisation and rather scornful of humankind.

I think it will remain like that for ever. I hope so. One thing is for sure, civilisation, whatever that is, will spread but it is doubtful it will ever really conquer this country. The Northern Territory is too fierce and proud for that. The Territory does not lend itself to the easy compromises of nicer, greener or better watered landscapes. This land is majestic and powerful. It is too rough and disdainful to be considered anything but a cruel master. Here you do not play games except at your own risk.

Yet, as this book will show, it can display touches of quite astonishing gentleness. When it does, the beauty it reveals is simply tremendous. There is really no other way to describe it. If I were asked what it is that I remember best and most of my years of

roaming the Territory's deep outback, I would have to answer that it is the absolute beauty and peace of some of the places I have visited.

There is nothing as vivid in my mind as driving a few hundred kilometres through what most people would consider terrible country and arriving at the end of a long hot day at a camping site that, if it were discovered, would become a promotional dream of any travel agent in Australia and overseas. Well, the Territory's parks are all like that.

While this book is about nature—in fact nature at its very best—it is also about the particular relationship that exists between Australia's original inhabitants, the Aborigines, and their land.

Here in the Northern Territory, Aboriginal culture, way of life, traditions and customs are not something that belongs just in history books or museums. They are living, and in many cases, thriving.

About one quarter of the Territory's population of 160 000 are Aborigines. While some are urban most are tribal, practising rituals and lore over 40 000 years old.

Aboriginal life in the Northern Territory is one of the land's best and most attractive assets. Where else can we find a civilisation as old as this?

Visitors should have special regard for this ancient culture. This includes respecting sacred sites or other sites of significance to Aborigines.

They exist in every park, providing added mystique to a land that is already nothing less than awesome.

Of course not all the human heritage associated with the Territory goes back that far. White Australian settlement has a short history by comparison—a little more than a hundred years. Still, the historical evidence is there and can be found around the place. Explorers, gold miners and drovers have all made their various contributions over the years, and helped to make the land what it is today. Without their efforts, there would never have been a Murranji Track, or an Overland Telegraph Line, or an

Arltunga gold field.

On a related topic, many of the Territory's parks contain areas that really are relics of prehistory. The cycads for instance, are the oldest living plants to be found on earth today. They date back to an era when dinosaurs roamed the earth. Some of the cycads that I have seen around the Territory have got to be at least a couple of thousands of years old. They are a living fossil. For some reason or other, flora and fauna that have disappeared elsewhere in the world continue to exist and survive here, which again makes this land very special. We all have a responsibility to make sure this situation continues. A great deal of that responsibility falls upon the visitors themselves. If a rare plant or animal is destroyed, then the line of succession may be so thin that it breaks, and then they are lost forever.

I should finish with a word of thanks to the Minister for Conservation in the Northern Territory, the Hon. Daryl Manzie, without whose support this book would not have seen the light of day.

A special mention should also be made of the NT Director of Conservation, Mr Col Fuller, who negotiated the dreaded bureaucracy to make sure that the book arrived at a safe shore.

And to two rangers in particular, Mr Derek Roff and Mr Frank Woerle, the major photographic contributors to this book, I offer my thanks for their vivid perceptions of this incredible land which make the book all that it is meant to be.

To bring all of these aspects together in one book like this, is no easy job. The Northern Territory Conservation Commission rangers themselves have not only provided the bulk of the information, but also the majority of the photographs used to illustrate the book. They know and understand the country extremely well, and that knowledge has been put to good use here. They obviously enjoy their work and it shows through. I am genuinely proud to be associated with all of them, because like them, I too love this land.

Les Hiddins

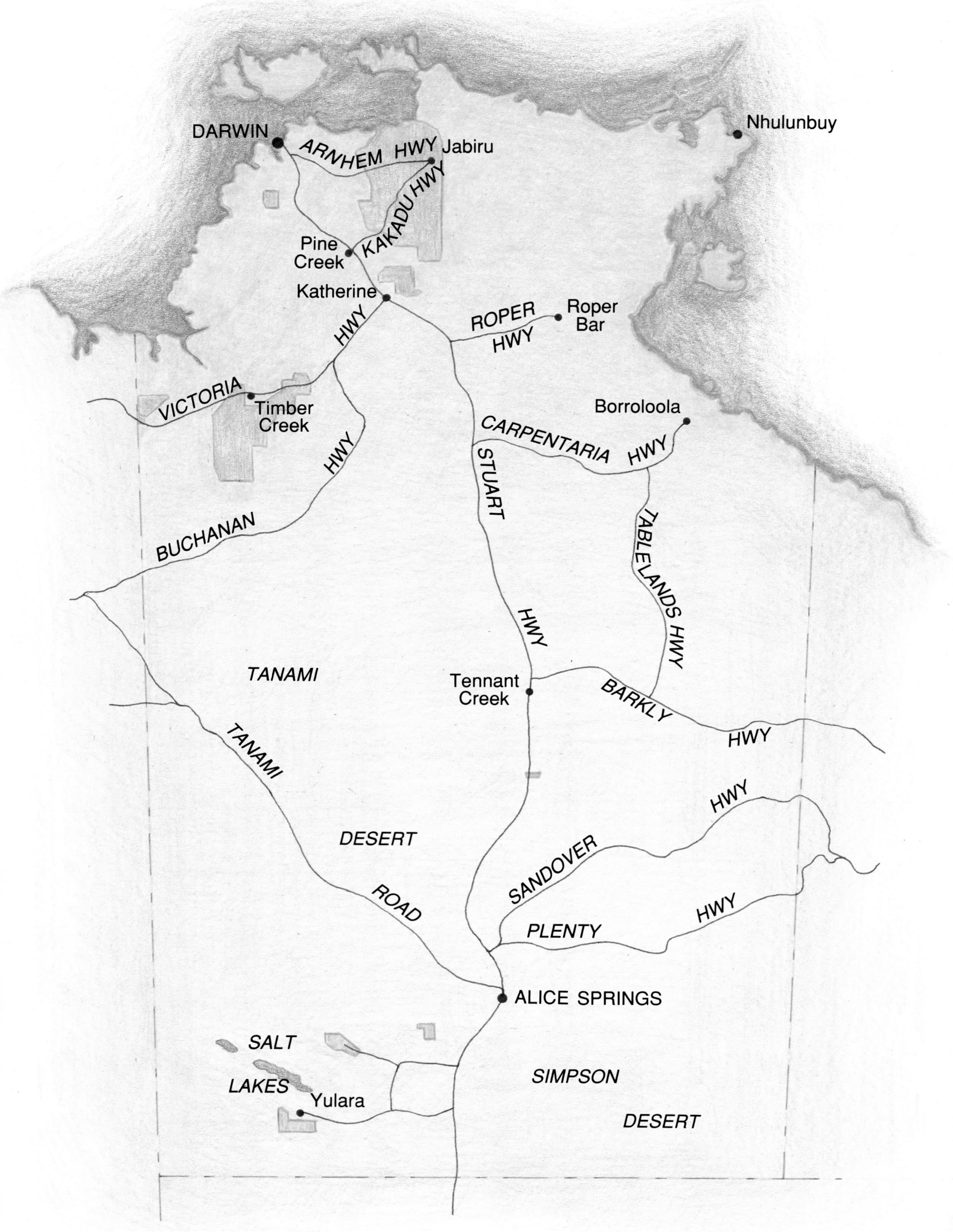

DARWIN

Nhulunbuy

ARNHEM HWY   Jabiru

KAKADU HWY

Pine
Creek

Katherine

ROPER
HWY

Roper
Bar

VICTORIA

HWY

Timber
Creek

CARPENTARIA   HWY

Borroloola

BUCHANAN

HWY

STUART

TABLELANDS HWY

TANAMI

HWY

TANAMI

Tennant
Creek

BARKLY

HWY

DESERT

ROAD

SANDOVER

HWY

PLENTY   HWY

ALICE SPRINGS

SALT

LAKES   Yulara

SIMPSON

DESERT

INTRODUCTION

*T*he Northern Territory is full of surprises. Look at it from the air and it could be the moon or, better yet, Mars. Red, barren and scarred, bizarre rock outcrops strewn at random like spent shrapnel, eccentric nature, it shows perhaps better than any region on earth the ravages of time and the unrelenting effects of a harsh environment.

The sun is an overpowering presence. People die here of thirst and exposure. Tourists who take foolish risks are asking for trouble. A young German who got confused at Kings Canyon was lost for some seven hours. Seven hours means nothing in Europe, but in Kings Canyon, it almost cost him his life.

Two other tourists, both young men, went walkabout in the Olgas from the Valley of the Winds to the Katatjuta Lookout. That is an easy three hour walk. Three hours means nothing in almost any part of the globe. But in Central Australia, they came close to perishing.

The sun, fierce and intransigent, has been the cause of too many deaths among visitors who believed they could translate their northern hemisphere experience to the Territory. It cannot be done. This is a whole new world demanding new rules.

And when it is not the sun, it is the distance (the Territory is 1.3 million square kilometres or bigger than several major European nations put together), raging flash floods, vast bushfires or cyclones. Above all, however, what matters in the Northern Territory is the intensity of isolation. This does not come about only, or even primarily, because there are just 160 000 people in such an immense region. It comes about mainly because of the environment.

A kinder environment, rolling green hills with plenty of forests, sparkling streams everywhere and snow peaks on the horizon would, I believe, tend to diminish and eventually cancel out any real sense of isolation brought about by scarce population.

But the Territory is not like that. The land is a monster that devours, not a loving mother nurturing her wayward child. As far as the eye can see, there are empty plains broken only by craggy red escarpments or bare ridges. It is not a land made for humans. Yet there are elements of tranquility that never cease to amaze. One moment there is nothing but the lash of burning sun on scraggly saltbush and withered hillocks. Next there is paradise. That is the nature of the Northern Territory.

Mangrove systems are an important breeding ground for prawns and other marine life.

PHOTOGRAPH BY TONY FORDE

10

TOP END

It is a land of contrast, this Top End of Australia.

In the dramatic 'green season' forbidding black storm clouds explode with summer lightning, thunderous waterfalls plummet from dizzying escarpments. Under the cloudless azure skies of the Dry, racing waters withdraw to the tranquility of chains of crystal clear pools.

Tropical vegetation, white sand beaches and flaming sunsets that mark the end of a perfect Top End day are but a few of the delights to be discovered in this very special country at the top of Australia's outback.

And at the very heart of the Top End, Kakadu National Park, a 6000 square kilometre wonderland protected forever under World Heritage Listing. Here the ferocious man-eating crocodile stalks his prey beneath fields of soft pink water-lilies, living in natural harmony with the succulent barramundi, the elegant Jabiru and the multitudinous magpie geese that live in colonies of thousands. Multi-hued parrots and cockatoos, the querulous brolga, the kookaburra and the kingfisher are just some of the 300 species of birds that call the Top End home ... more than half of all species in Australia.

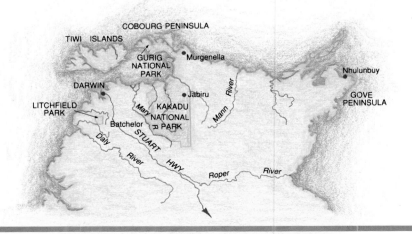

A spectacular aerial view of the northern coastline, Alcaro Bay, Arnhem Land.

PHOTOGRAPH BY PETER JARVER

12

GURIG
NATIONAL PARK
(COBOURG PENINSULA)

Cobourg Peninsula, on the western tip of Arnhem Land, is a treasure-trove of undiscovered riches. It combines spectacular scenery with adventure, history with timelessness. There is nothing like it anywhere in the world.

The peninsula, a gnarled finger of land jutting out into the Arafura Sea, is in fact the 2207 square kilometre Gurig National Park.

It has everything: coves, inlets and endless beaches of peerless beauty, a sea teeming with fish, forests full of big game, a staggering variety of birdlife, and, perhaps above all, history.

For this is the place where the burgeoning, aggressive, pushing European civilisation was forced to concede defeat.

The symbol of that defeat, the Waterloo of British expansion into northern Australia, is to be found in the Victoria settlement at Port Essington. It is difficult to imagine a more idyllic setting. Port Essington is a tropical retreat, a place of wonder, a Javanese inland bay without coconut trees.

I sailed there one October morning with two NT Conservation Commission rangers. The landing pier consists of a wooden platform extending from the coarse sandy shore well into the sea. Visitors are greeted by the smoke-blackened ruins, which having resisted the best endeavours of man and nature, stand intact in their bleak majesty.

I stood for a long time beside the collapsed walls and basements, and marvelled at the awesome audacity and glorious idiocy of the settlers and those who had sent them there in 1838.

They faced no extreme perils such as had been encountered by other explorers and settlers elsewhere. There was no dangerous foe to vanquish through heroic feats of arms. Indeed if the ostensible reason they had been put there was to stop the French or Germans from setting foot on the land, they were soon disillusioned. A French ship visited them in 1839, took a long look at the place, shared a bottle of cognac and several of rancid Bordeaux wine with the officers, and left them never to return.

The settlers were defeated only by nature, but nature does not offer clues for their demise, certainly not at first sight.

The exquisite blue seas and forest-fringed white beaches, fleecy clouds scudding above tall eucalypts and exotic palms, the

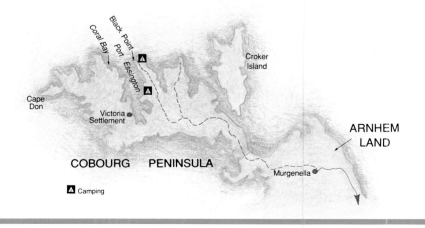

silent breaking of surf—none of those things seemed hostile.

Neither were the native blacks, the Madjunbalmi Aborigines, who met the pale newcomers with the same indifferent equanimity with which they had met the Macassan fishermen in search of trepang perhaps 200 years before the Europeans arrived.

There is a slight rise from the beach to the settlement itself. It is an easy walk up a sandy path shaded by trees. Yet I was sweating profusely by the time we reached the low promontory where Captain Gordon Bremer, the settlement's first governor, had his home erected. I was also thirsty and this is of course the clue to the settlement's failure.

The knoll was a perfect spot for a picnic. Behind were the stone works of the settlement, flawlessly carved by the stonemasons of an age long gone. Ahead was a cove, a small sheltered bay of waters so vividly blue that they appeared to jump and blend with the mangled forest.

But one thing was missing in an otherwise perfect setting. There were no clear rivulets singing their way into the sea. No creeks, no rivers, no lakes. There was no drinking water anywhere. The settlers had a choice of several far more suitable locations within a ten kilometre radius to establish themselves. But they settled here, an unforgiving and cruel place behind a facade of indescribable beauty.

And here they dug three deep wells, essentially underwater storage tanks for monsoonal rains. Otherwise they had no water. None at all. They quarried the unyielding cliff face for lime and carved tonnes of rocks into building blocks. They toiled day and night for eleven long years and, being only human beings, many died.

For there is no food either unless one happens to be an expert in bushcraft. They certainly were not. Mostly they were decent English folk probably much more at home in the Russian steppes than here. The Aborigines probably watched them starve in some amazement. There was plenty of food around for those who knew where to find it. In any case their herculean tasks cannot be understood except in the context of the times. All they left were the ruins and the memories.

Perhaps significantly, the settlers established a cemetery for their dead adjacent to their sole garden in swampy ground near the beach.

One of the graves bears a fairly recent inscription. 'In loving memory of Emma Lambrick and child, wife of Lieutenant Lambrick of Hobart.'

Their remains lie underground, the debris of colonial dreams and the symbol of a nation's universal destiny. I wondered briefly if Mrs Lambrick thought at all about the breathtaking surroundings she was leaving behind as she died.

It was a melancholy experience visiting the forlorn ruins of the Victoria settlement. But the experience should not be missed because it tells so much about the Northern Territory.

It is everywhere the same. First a shock of beauty followed by failure and harsh struggle. The truly astonishing loveliness of the seas and the land coupled to fearful forces that perhaps only the Aborigines, and they dimly, can understand. Forces like cyclones which regularly sweep in from the Arafura Sea destroying everything in their path.

Victoria was razed to the ground in 1839, just one year after establishment. The rangers at Black Point, where visitors should report before embarking on their exploration, spoke prosaically about 'the possibility of a big blow this year'.

And cyclones are not the only hazard. Large saltwater crocodiles cruise sedately in the incomparable estuaries and mangroves of the vast peninsula.

There are also sharks in the waters around and dolphins galore pirouetting high on the boat's surge.

And it is a fishermen's paradise. Swing a line over the side and haul in a big mackerel for your barbecue lunch. Or, if your taste ranges to coral trout, by all means sail to the reef and catch one. In fact you might just prefer snapper, barramundi, or glass-eyed perch.

The seas around Cobourg abound with a

14

PHOTOGRAPH BY
FRANK WOERLE

Tropical cyclone Max crosses over the Cobourg Peninsula on its journey toward Darwin.

PHOTOGRAPH BY PETER JARVER

Remains of the married quarters at Victoria Settlement; a vivid reminder of the isolation and hardship endured by early settlers in the Northern Territory.

Coastal wild-flowers are salt tolerant and grow in beach sand. Their existence on the beach dunes serves to hold the sand in place during harsh winds.

Ximenia belongs to the citrus family and is known to exist in only three locations. It is a much desired delicacy of the Aboriginal people.

Kernels of the pandanus fruit are difficult to extract, but have a pleasant nutty flavour.

PHOTOGRAPHS BY FRANK WOERLE

16

*M*angrove community at low tide, Cobourg Peninsula.

rich variety of species. They are all waiting to be fished.

There are also five kinds of turtle, from flat-backs to loggerheads. Dugongs or sea cows visit the area as well but I did not see any and I believe their numbers are not great.

More important for sybarites with jaded palates are the banks of fresh and totally uncontaminated oysters. A sturdy knife and a dash of lemon are all that is needed for a perfect appetiser.

From Victoria to Coral Bay is only a brief sail but the hop-and-step is a must. The bay is a blue, green and gold jewel trapped by nature to lure weary travellers and cast a spell upon them. It is as far away from the stresses and strains of modern living as it is possible to get.

But Cobourg is not only the bewitching seas and shores. It is a large land park where big-game hunters can have their day.

Banteng or Bali cattle and wide-horned buffalo, both introduced for food by the British last century, roam wild. They adapted to the new land remarkably well and proliferated in great numbers. Unfortunately they are feral animals that cause a great deal of environmental damage and carry diseases such as brucellosis and tuberculosis. Some must therefore be destroyed.

There are well-organised and highly controlled safaris that, on arrangement with the Aboriginal traditional owners, engage in selected shooting of animals.

A description of the region cannot escape mention of its geography. The Aborigines, who own most of the park and manage it jointly with the NT Conservation Commission, say the park was born in a single act of creation. They have invested the rock formations along the coast with great significance.

Many of the rocks are 'sacred/secret and/ or dangerous' and others are associated with ancestral beings of the 'Dreamtime'.

Port Essington for example is the site of Banibuladjang, the Greenback Turtle Dreaming Site. Here turtles can be multiplied by rubbing two special rocks which represent turtles. But take care with this fertility rite, for if the rocks are rubbed too hard a deadly cyclone may result.

The point here of course is that the original inhabitants of the Gurig National Park are not just owners/managers. They are an integral part of the park and one of its best and most attractive assets.

Their stories and traditions, dating back countless generations, are one of the most fascinating mixtures of myth and reality, blending cataclysmic geological events with everyday life. Story telling around a flickering fire reflected wanly on the calm surf and in the black forest is an unforgettable experience.

There is 'gargul gunak', the dominant eucalypt vegetation of the peninsula which is good because it is a source of food and medicine. Others are bad: 'Bani bunji', a patch of rainforest where an evil spirit lives, or 'Arragaladdi', two hills with sacred banyan trees. Banyan trees are normally considered benign by the Aborigines but, for some reason, not in this area where they are considered highly dangerous and capable of causing great physical damage.

Finally, with your senses saturated by so much seen, felt and heard, take a sailing trip to Cape Don on the foremost western tip of the park.

Cape Don is the site of a tall lighthouse built in 1916 along with two homes, now included in the Heritage Listing for their architectural and historical value.

The place is important for two reasons. The first is that the lighthouse and homes were built while the Great War raged in Europe and the Middle East, killing millions and extinguishing the bright lights of Western civilisation almost everywhere.

They were built against enormous odds— the materials were shipped all the way from Melbourne—in one of the most desolate and isolated spots on earth. If that does not constitute a touching and courageous affirmation of faith in the future, I do not know what does.

The second is that Cape Don could be made into an ideal retreat. One of the rambling homes, built in classic pre-war tropical colonial style, is somewhat dilapidated but not beyond repair.

ome mangrove species establish themselves by vertical floating seedlings carried by the tides. The seeds actually germinate on the tree, before dropping into the water.

PHOTOGRAPH BY TONY FORDE

In fact the temptation is to keep Cobourg as something of a pristine exhibit, never to be touched and most certainly never to be ravaged by the wreckage of industrial effluent.

Looking at the luxuriant vegetation and bright blue waters of Coral Bay, I told one of the rangers that, one day, perhaps in the not too distant future, the bay would be dotted with dozens of yachts and pleasure craft from all points of the globe. Sadly, the ranger agreed with my prophecy.

But the park's attraction consists of not only the things I have mentioned—fishing, hunting, sailing and sight seeing. Its isolation and remoteness have made Cobourg one of the best kept secrets in Australia and, in this age of vast international tourism, in the world. Where else can one retreat in time as well as in geography? Where else can the weary traveller buy this immense peace in the midst of stunning beauty?

At present remoteness and isolation are likely to remain, at least in the short term. Access is mainly by sea and air. Road travel is difficult and requires permits from traditional Aboriginal owners through the Northern Land Council.

The Gurig National Park was declared only in 1981. It is therefore a very new park where facilities are scarce or simply non-existent. It is very much a do-your-own-thing affair which of course adds to the charm but not necessarily to the comfort.

The rangers at Black Point or at Cape Don are helpful and professional. As a matter of courtesy as well as for your own safety, let them know you are in the area and ask them the location of camping spots. You will save them and yourself some bother by showing a little common sense.

Having done that, go ahead and enjoy yourself. It is difficult not to in this gem of a place.

The Murgenella plains have now fully recovered from buffalo damage and are an important breeding and feeding area for magpie geese and other water fowl.

PHOTOGRAPH BY FRANK WOERLE

20

MURGENELLA

Say Murgenella. Let the syllables roll off your tongue bringing with them the salty breeze of Mur and the exotic romance of Genella. Now you have Murgenella.

It is in Arnhem Land, just east of and adjacent to the Cobourg Peninsula. Murgenella is Aboriginal land, hazy from the air, the mangroves of the Mini-Mini River system dominating the landscape, green and blue, with great shining expanses during the welcome monsoon rains.

But the one thing that really distinguishes the Murgenella coast from any other shoreline, in the Territory or elsewhere, cannot be seen from the air, certainly not with any sense of detail or appreciation of its uniqueness.

It is the marvellous 25 000-year-old sand dunes, giant mounds held together by dwarf wattle and lording it over an impressive coastline. And the seas here are, as at Cobourg, glass-clear and spotted by banks of fresh oysters and grey and brown rocks. The forest that fringes most of the vast beach has not been burned for a generation. It has recovered from the earlier ravages and is at a stage preceding rainforest. Immaculate trees interspersed by large patches of palms, paperbarks and native cypresses. Listen carefully: this is paradise.

It was raining heavily when I visited the dunes, the second oldest in the world. The seas were gun-metal grey and broken only by the occasional foamy ripple. Behind me was the dark-green forest, under my feet the hard-soft feel of the wet sand caressed by a blanket of stunted wattle. An amazing littoral of cliffs, little ravines, hidden coves, beaches and bays stretched as far as the eye could see. And not a single human being, no one, in the whole wilderness. Only a large crocodile swimming out to sea disturbed the absolute peace.

Next day dawned tropical blue and sunny. Fishing is splendid. Skinny, Spanish flag, coral trout, turrum, barracuda, reef cod and mackerel were among the delicious fish that quickly filled a large drum. A particularly attractive hidden cove, with a freshwater stream fringed by pandanus, provided the ideal spot for a delicious meal of grilled fish washed down by cold beer. The sunset splashed clouds, sea and sand dunes with a kaleidoscope of colour. It was a rare moment. This is perfection, the world that cynics claim does not exist.

Opposite is Croker Island which, like

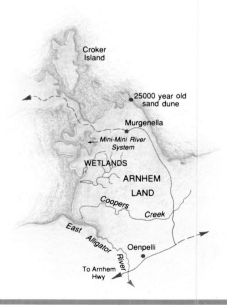

Majestic cliffs on the east coast of Murgenella.

The cattle egret derives its name from its habit of feeding on parasites found on the backs of cattle and buffalo.

The Murgenella sand dunes began to form approximately 25 000 years ago ... some of the oldest sand dunes in the world.

Wild grapes (Cayratia terisolia) are native to Australia and highly desirable bush tucker. If eaten to excess they leave an alkaline taste in the mouth.

PHOTOGRAPHS BY FRANK WOERLE

Murgenella, is fully owned by the Aborigines. It beckoned with a quiet beauty reminiscent of islands under the sun, far away, exotic and never to be touched.

But the sand and sea are just one aspect of this magical piece of land. The Mini-Mini mangrove delta is a haven of crabs, barramundi and other aquatic life. It literally teems with fish and birds barely disturbed by the lazy purr of an outboard motor.

A little to the south are the wetlands, as good as any in the Top End and better than most. Until recently they were a marsh, a giant mudbath for buffaloes and feral pigs. But following the eradication of both animals the wetlands are well advanced in the process of rehabilitation. Already delicate waterlilies have made their first timid appearance and the floodplains are smiling.

As is the case with so many other parks in the Territory, Murgenella is quite simply a staggeringly beautiful area that remains blissfully undiscovered.

If I were to define its unbelievable charm with one word, I would use contrast. For Murgenella is a piece of land full of contrast. There is the shoreline, pristine and beautiful beyond words. Then there are mangrove swamps calling to be explored and fished. The rainforests, cool, untouched, beckoning. And finally, the floodplains stretching vast distances and as calmly majestic as those of Kakadu.

Access is difficult. First a Northern Land Council permit is needed because this is Aboriginal land. It takes about one hour to fly there from Darwin. The road leads to Jabiru, in the heart of Kakadu, and then across the East Alligator River to Oenpelli and north to Murgenella itself. The East Alligator is often impassable during the Wet and, in any case, the numbers of cars travelling to Murgenella and Cobourg (about 120 kilometres away) are restricted to 10–15 per week.

The traditional owners are at present negotiating the possibility of opening up the area to tourism. Conservation Commission rangers manage it as if it were a park but have no authority. The future of this extraordinarily attractive region will remain unclear until a firm understanding or agreement is reached between the various interests.

One thing is for certain, however: Murgenella demands care. It is simply exquisite.

*A*t sunrise on Murgenella Creek, the soft lighted shadows on a small pool present a picture of total serenity.

A secluded waterfall and popular swimming spot amongst the rainforest on Melville Island.

PHOTOGRAPH BY FRANK WOERLE

26

TIWI ISLANDS

*M*elville and Bathurst Islands are twin jewels that Tiwi Aborigines call home.

A short flight north of Darwin, they are nevertheless a world apart from the Australian mainland. For here you will sniff the first pungent aroma of the Asia–Pacific rim and its exotic life. You will be transported into an era that you thought had disappeared. And you will witness traditions and customs of a proud Aboriginal race that looks the 21st century in the eye. A race so unafraid and confident that it brings joy to the soul. I first saw Melville Island from the air. Our single engine plane flew very low to stay below heavy clouds laden with rain. It was buffeted by the winds as it made its approach from the grey seas rippled with white.

Suddenly the island appeared straight ahead. My senses were jarred. I wanted to hold this moment and not let it pass. Under the frail fuselage and beyond the rain-streaked windows was a scene of such rare beauty that it should have been shared by the spirit, not the physical senses.

The island unfolded sinuously, hundreds of white beaches crowned by dense forest and devoid of any sign of human habitation. Only the surf breaking silently under the dark skies and the murmur of the foliage on the wind.

This was the beginning of time. Here is where God rehearsed the earth and, having succeeded, went ahead with the rest.

Now I understood the Tiwi story about Mudangkala, the legendary woman who created the islands. She was an old blind woman who arose from the ground carrying three babies in her arms. There was nothing in the landscape. It was a barren piece of earth. But as she crawled, she carved a narrow channel between Bathurst and Melville Islands and the darkness filled with seawater and plants and animals. Little could Mudangkala have imagined that the channel, the Aspley Strait, subject to huge tidal forces, could be turned into a vast hydroelectric station providing power for industry and domestic use in the islands and elsewhere. There is a proposal to do precisely that at present.

Before Mudangkala went back into the ground she had left paradise for her children. One of them, Purakapali, fought the Moon Man, Tjapara, with forked sticks creating a legend that later inspired the superb Tiwi carving.

Mudangkala's descendants form special groups called Imunga. They are the equivalent of Scottish clans but here clan groupings are passed from the mother, not from the father. Land owning, on the other hand, is patrilineal. The parallel system works well. It can be said that cultural and social affairs are controlled by women while economic affairs are the responsibility of men.

A little later the plane landed at Pickertaramoor, a small strip in the southern part of the island servicing a sprawling pine plantation.

Pickertaramoor is a charming cluster of old forestry homes encircled by rainforest. Nearby is a beautiful waterfall and picnic grounds set like a peaceful oasis amidst riotous vegetation. A little beyond, the pines begin. They have come a long way, mainly from the torrid Caribbean, and have adapted to their new home well. One day they will give the Tiwis a good income and,

BATHURST ISLAND — Pularumpi — Milikapiti — Paru — Nguiu — MELVILLE ISLAND — Pickertarmoor

PHOTOGRAPH BY FRANK WOERLE

ukamani burial poles on Melville Island are carved with the life story of the person they commemorate.

in the meantime, they are a tourist attraction in themselves.

About 40 kilometres from Pickertaramoor is Turacumbie Falls, a place of tranquillity and peace. Clear waters tumble between rocks cascading free after a brief struggle with ancient tree roots and curious ferns. The falls are the home of the well-known Territory family, the Tipilouras, all members of the Wulirangkuwu clan. Stanley Tipiloura is a Labor parliamentarian in the Northern Territory's Legislative Assembly. His brother Bernard is a board member with the NT Conservation Commission.

From there it is only a short side trip to the Tiwi burial sites at Milikapiti and its fantastic collection of Totem poles. Many of the designs on the Totems are masterpieces of carving and give visitors a clear idea of the Tiwis' artistic abilities. It is that ability that has created a burgeoning industry in the islands. Tiwi designs, traditionally used on ceremonial objects, are rapidly gaining pride of place in the international fashion world as more and more people become acquainted with the delicate motifs and striking colours that have already made them world famous.

Tiwi pottery and Tiwi pima wood carving have not yet been as widely recognised as the fashion designs but they are also about to break into the national and international

scene because they are both world class.

But Milikapiti (Snake Bay) has a lot more to offer. It has one of the most impressive harbours I have seen and its beauty does justice to the little township perched on its shores. Its equivalent in Bathurst is Nguiu, which began as a Catholic Mission in 1911 and has developed to a progressive community of more than 1200 people.

The road from Milikapiti to Pirlangimpi (sometimes known as Garden Point or Pulatumpi) is good even under the heavy monsoonal rains and will take you through imposing pine forests. A couple of rivers have amazing small forests of nipa palms that, as far as I am aware, originated in Papua New Guinea and do not grow anywhere on the Australian mainland.

Pirlangimpi is well worth visiting for at least three good reasons: it has an exquisite shoreline, it is the home of some of Australia's best footballers, and, nearby, are the remnants of Britain's failure to establish a settlement here.

The beaches are magnificent and inviting. As is so often the case in the Top End, the eyes cannot wholly encompass the beauty of these places. One day they will be developed and visitors will flock because almost nowhere else in the world can they find what sites like Pirlangimpi offer in such abundance. This is virgin country. The sand, sea and forests are the same as they

have been for thousands of years.

Whenever I come to places like this I am overwhelmed by a melancholy feeling that no one should be told they exist. I want them only for myself, unspoilt and untouched, but I know it cannot be.

I am almost certain the grand old man of football, Cyril Rioli, who lives at Pirlangimpi, would agree with that assessment. His neat cottage is full of trophies, mute witnesses of the great sporting feats with which the Rioli name is associated. They have institutionalised Australian Rules Football, not just in Bathurst and Melville Islands but in Darwin.

Football is not quite as important as the Catholic Faith here but is not far behind. It is a pleasure to watch these strong and lithe youngsters manipulate a football with a skill that would be the envy of professionals in Melbourne or Adelaide. The annual fixture at Bathurst has become a major Northern Territory event attended by the Administrator and many Darwinians who fly there for a sporting feast.

Across the bay is a heavily wooded promontory. It looks inoffensive enough, but, in fact, it is the site of Fort Dundas, a place of hell for Captain Gordon Bremer of the Royal Navy and his people who in 1824 attempted to establish a settlement there. Relations between the newcomers and the proud Tiwis were not good. They were not even indifferent as in the Victoria settlement at Port Essington. Clashes occurred and while the Tiwis demonstrated a healthy regard for firearms, the regard did not stop them from continuous harassment of the pale settlers. Four years later, the British left. Their ruins, now almost totally covered by the jungle, stand in bleak testimony of their attempt.

The Tiwis did not see war again until February 1942 when the Japanese bombed the islands on their way to Darwin. It was strafed by enemy aircraft, the first Japanese bullets fired against Australians in Australia.

A Catholic missionary based there was the first to radio the news of a vast Japanese air fleet approaching the town. Unfortunately, the authorities in Darwin chose to ignore the desperate radio message. The consequences were devastating. Hundreds of residents were killed, the air force base destroyed, and many ships anchored in the Darwin port sunk. It was the first enemy attack on Australian soil. A Tiwi, Matthias Ulungura, a short time later, captured a Japanese pilot who crash landed on Melville Island.

The islands therefore are not just precious natural gems, they are the ancient repositories of history and traditions as old as humanity.

The islanders have looked at the potential benefits from tourism and have made their first timid entry into this activity. The Barra Lodge on Bathurst Island is a superb lodge that combines comfort with the ruggedness of bush life. Placed on the beach, it offers visitors the rare spectacle of wild crocodiles coming into the sand to be fed. There is no doubt that as Bathurst and Melville Islands are discovered, there will be many more visitors who will want to see the marvels they offer. At present a small airline, Tiwi Tours, operates a service from Darwin. Visitors can take a full day tour or stay overnight camping under tents.

The islands are Aboriginal land under the administration of the Tiwi Land Council formed in 1977. A permit is needed to gain access, but the procedure is not difficult and the friendly islanders welcome visitors. All they ask is that, in turn, their traditions and the land that has been their home forever are treated with respect.

The smiling face of a young Islander.

PHOTOGRAPH BY DAVID SILVA

Limestone pillars, carved by wind and water, Cape Arnhem coast.

PHOTOGRAPH BY DEREK ROFF

GOVE PENINSULA

*F*irst came the Aborigines. The tall, lithe black men and women and their brood broke through the land of swamps, pandanus and eucalypts to arrive at their destination.

They probably did not care much about the stunning beauty of the land they were about to settle. The unending sand dunes, forested shores and delicate beaches decorated by rocks like pearls. Survival was uppermost and beauty, in itself, does not feed hungry mouths.

But here there was plenty of food as well. Turtles, oysters and all kinds of fish. Wild berries and fruit. Wallabies and crocodiles. Birds. They were abundant, put on the land and in the seas by a generous provider who did not want these puny intruders to die.

They did not. Here in the Gove Peninsula in east Arnhem Land, they found a home so rich and plentiful that very soon it allowed them to multiply and become masters of their own lives. Not for them, not ever, the capricious cruelty of the desert or the devastating whims of nature. They lacked nothing.

For many thousands of years they and their descendants carved a niche in history, one that in all likelihood saw less systematic brutality and far less conflict than other societies elsewhere.

Then in 1632, with Europe submerged in the last of the great wars of religion, a Dutchman, Willem van Colster, in the *Arnhem*, became the first white man to sight the area. But he and his scurvy-ridden crew left no traces.

Neither did the Macassan fishermen who came here for trepang or the pathetic British attempts to establish a settlement in northern Australia in the 1800s. They came and went practically unnoticed and certainly unlamented.

Much, much later, the missionaries arrived bringing Christianity and a way of life that the native inhabitants easily superimposed on their own beliefs. Traders followed and then serious students of anthropology became fascinated by this corner of Utopia.

During World War 2, an air squadron was based on the peninsula's northernmost tip. A well-known and well-liked fighter pilot, William Gove, who died during a mission in New Guinea, gave the peninsula its name. But the war did not change anything. The substance of the area and the people remained intact.

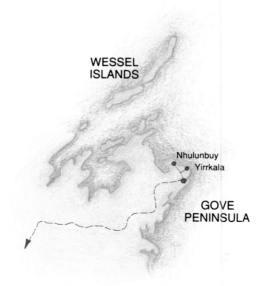

WESSEL
ISLANDS

Nhulunbuy
Yirrkala

GOVE
PENINSULA

PHOTOGRAPH BY FRANK WOERLE

Trepang have been collected by Macassan people for hundreds of years as a much sought after delicacy. Mudcrabs are found along the entire northern coastline. As well as being good bush tucker, they have a high commercial value.

Finally the miners came. Soon things changed. A new town, Nhulunbuy, was created where only wilderness had existed. Huge machines excavated the crimson earth. A massive factory was built on the edge of turquoise waters. Civilisation had arrived.

The descendants of that first group of Aborigines fought back. In 1969, the Gumatj leaders organised a petition against the miners, Nabalco, a consortium of Swiss and Australian companies. They were following the example of another tribe, the Gurindji, who in 1967 had walked off Wave Hill to protest at working conditions and demand their own land.

Together, the actions of the Gumatj and Gurindji eventually gave way to land rights in 1976. Nabalco pays handsome royalties to the Aborigines and the company's record, not only in its relationship with the native inhabitants but also in the rehabilitation of the land, is excellent.

In any case the mine's operations,

extensive as they are, have hardly detracted from the quintessential beauty of the area. It remains largely as it was those thousands of years ago when humans first appeared.

Nhulunbuy's beaches need no introduction. They are justly renowned as some of the most attractive shorelines in Australia.

But nothing, not even Nhulunbuy's pristine sands, can prepare the visitor for the stretch of coast to the east, between Cape Arnhem and Port Bradshaw. It is here that the ancient gods established Nirvana long before Heaven was created.

Visitors leave the bitumen road at the airport, about 11 kilometres south of Nhulunbuy, and enter a thick forest of stringybarks and stunted *Livistona* palms. This is strictly four-wheel drive country with a track that would have been extremely difficult for the bullock teams of the past to negotiate.

Then quite suddenly the first sand dunes appear and, beyond, a most spectacular

*T*win Eagles
Beach,
Arnhem Coast.
Picturesque white
sandy beaches are
only part of the
magical attraction
of Gove.

PHOTOGRAPH BY DEREK ROFF

33

PHOTOGRAPH BY FRANK WOERLE

Echidnas are monotremes and their main diet is termites.

shoreline. The sea shines with iridescent tiny blue stars that crash with a soft murmur against the beach's fine snow-white powder. Only the breeze and the surf break the chant of galahs feeding on casuarinas and terns skipping out of the way.

The sheer transluscence of the water soothes the eyes and the mind. A large fish leaps high in the air curious at the newcomers. The reef smiles contentedly. Here is a world that has not changed for thousands of years.

Not a single high rise building and no sign of human habitation anywhere. Just the magnificent dunes interspersed by rocky outcrops so weathered that they look like delicate oyster platters on top of one another.

A fat turtle waddles lazily out to sea. Its dark shadow lingers beneath the turquoise water for an eternity. It leaves behind a large log brought here from far shores by the currents. There are a few shrivelled coconuts around. If they miss their exotic

homes it is only as the old miss familiar possessions and places, not like the young hankering for a hurried future.

Here and there are nests built by white-breasted eagles high on the cliffs away from predatory dingoes and crocodiles.

At Cave Beach, a small cove where a stream sings its way into the sea, a clump of paperbark trees blends into limestone rocks and sand. This was never meant to be on earth. It was meant only as a rehearsal of Paradise but left here by a forgetful Creator.

The experience is quite simply unforgettable. On the way back to Nhulunbuy, the track winds on the edge of a very large pandanus forest, an emerald jewel forbidden to any but the brave and resourceful.

The Gumatj claim that only those who have been initiated into the world of the Spirits are allowed into this forest. What they mean is that this land is dangerous. There are crocodiles in the swamps and snakes. It is easy to get lost in the

impenetrable tangle of vines, trees, pandanus palms and mangrove scrub. But its forbidding nature adds to its attraction. This is the magical land of witches and warlocks, of dragons and knights and damsels.

From the blue-water marlin to mackerel, from reef trout to cod, trevally, barracuda, turrum and barramundi, the sea teems with all kinds of fish. And the islands nearby provide idyllic surroundings for visiting fishermen.

Just imagine hooking skinny all day and retiring to an improbable cove fringed by forest to watch the sunset with the delicious aroma of grilled fish wafting around you.

The weather is balmy all year round although during the monsoon season storms and sometimes violent cyclones lash the region.

A word of warning here. This is all Aboriginal land and a permit is required from the owners. The process is to write to the Permits Officer, Bureau of the Northern Land Council at PO Box 820, Nhulunbuy, and request an application form. The islanders ask for little. They do not want visitors to leave a mess behind. It is not an unreasonable request.

Access is mainly by sea and air. Nhulunbuy is about 650 kilometres east of Darwin and there are well established airlines that do the trip regularly.

It is also possible to journey by four-wheel drive from Katherine to Nhulunbuy but the track is difficult and, again, a permit from the NLC is needed. Nowadays the trip from Katherine takes about 14 hours of hard driving. During the Wet, a number of rivers make the road impassable. The worst obstacle is the Goyder River which is about 50 metres wide and has a very rough rocky bed between steep banks. And there are crocodiles here.

But perhaps that is what makes this track one of the best four-wheel drive adventures in Australia. The scenery, encompassing as it does escarpments, heavily wooded country and fine rivers, is an added incentive for enthusiasts.

Gove is a must. It is an unspoilt corner of Australia where some powerful magician once stepped in and waved his wand. Having done the trick he then forgot to make the land revert to monotony.

And it has not yet been discovered. Except by you.

Government House. This is the Administrator's (governor in the States) residence in Darwin. It witnessed the Territory's own Rum Rebellion in 1918 when an unruly mob assaulted the building and forced Administrator Gilruth out of the Territory. The residence suffered serious damage from the Japanese bombing of February 19, 1942 but has been carefully restored.

PHOTOGRAPH BY CONSERVATION COMMISSION

DARWIN

The city of Darwin was first named Port Darwin by John Lort Stokes, commander of the *Beagle*, on 9 September 1839. Stokes thought he would pay tribute to an old friend, Charles Darwin, who had been a ship's companion on a previous voyage to South America. Darwin, who was to publish his monumental *Origin of the Species* some 20 years later, was not on board this time and had not yet acquired fame. But now his name would live forever in this large and beautiful harbour fringed by deep green mangroves and clear beaches.

There would be no European presence here for many years, not until 1869, when the South Australian Government sent its Surveyor General, George Goyder, to select and survey a site in the north for such a settlement. The party met the area's Aboriginal owners, the Larrakia, who resented the newcomers and killed one of the party's draftsmen, J. W. Bennett. Here, like elsewhere in the Northern Territory, there was at first resistance to the newcomers, and then an accommodation of this strange new civilisation. But the process took much longer than in the rest of Australia, because Darwin remained an isolated and remote outpost of European settlement until well after World War 2.

Goyder left behind a town plan fashioned along Adelaide's grid lines, which survives to this day and makes up the city centre. The streets here are all named after the original surveyors: Smith (part of which is now a mall), Bennett, MacLachlan, Knuckey, Woods, McMinn and Mitchell.

The following year, in October 1870, the SA Government started construction of the Overland Telegraph from Port Augusta to Darwin, and this was really the beginning of the city. Gold was discovered during construction and there was a minor gold rush. The discovery of gold did not do for Darwin and for the Northern Territory what it had done for New South Wales, Victoria and Western Australia. The climate here was too hard, the country unremittingly hostile, and there was never much gold to go around anyway. The rush petered off, leaving South Australia in charge of a new colonial settlement that it had neither the resources nor the will to develop.

At one stage in the late 1870s, the rush attracted just over 7000 Chinese. The first boatload of hopefuls came from Singapore and there was subsequent emigration from Hsi Chian River region in China, Kwantung province and Hong Kong. They joined Cingalese (Sinhalese), Malays, Japanese, Indonesians and Filipinos (Manilamen), vastly outnumbering the few hundred Europeans in Darwin (then called Palmerston). By 1890, the total non-Aboriginal population of the Territory was

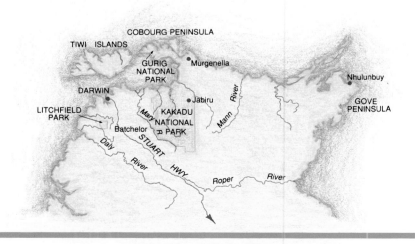

5366, of whom 4141 were Chinese and 216 other Asians. But by 1910, due to restrictions on the Chinese and Asians generally, the non-Aboriginal population had dwindled to 2846, of whom only 1182 were Europeans.

In turn, the Asians were outnumbered by the native tribes, mainly Larrakia, Wagait and Brinkin, although Aboriginal presence in the tiny urban settlement was nowhere near as noticeable as that of the Asians. The first formal assessments of the Territory Aboriginal population were attempted in 1891 and 1901. These censuses, if such they can be called, came up with an Aboriginal population of between 21 000 and 23 000 respectively, although their accuracy is highly questionable.

Port Darwin at the turn of the century was a collection of shacks precariously perched on the edge of the Arafura Sea. A cyclone destroyed what there was of it in 1897, but reconstruction did not take long because there was so little to reconstruct.

Perhaps one of the most telling descriptions of Darwin at the time was made by a visiting politician, Senator MacDougall, in 1912, who described the settlement as 'one of the most squalid, contemptible places I ever saw'. His colleague in the House of Representatives, Granville Ryrie, said that 'the country in and around Darwin will not feed a bandicoot'.

For his part, Administrator John Gilruth's secretary, Carey, wrote in 1912 that 'he (Gilruth) found Darwin a slovenly township with a "Chinatown" in which conditions were appalling from a public health point of view, with rubbish lying everywhere and malaria far more prevalent than was desirable'.

It was not a pleasant town or one that most Australians in the mythical 'south' cared about or had even heard mentioned. The streets turned to mud in the Wet and to dust in the Dry. Spear grass grew wild in the footpaths, such as they were. And apart from some frangipani, hibiscus, poincianas, and coconut trees, the only vegetation was typical Top End scrub.

It was a rigidly segregated frontier town, with the Chinese and other Asians in Chinatown (now Cavanagh Street), the blacks at Lameroo Beach below the Esplanade and at Kahlin Compound nearby, and whites in Smith and Mitchell streets and in the Esplanade. The 'coloured', accepted neither by Aborigines, Asians nor whites, lived near the Police Barracks in what is now Stuart Park. Only in 1938 did segregation start to break down after an enterprising and courageous Chinese, George Lim, bought a shop in Smith Street against dire warnings he could not succeed trading in the white man's area. He did, and the Lims prospered. One, Alec Fong Lim, was to become a very popular Lord Mayor of Darwin in the 1980s (Lake Alexander is named after him).

Goldmining nearby, pearling, fishing and cattle were some of the few productive activities undertaken at the time. Otherwise, most of the well-off Europeans were government officials or telegraph employees. The not so well-off whites were largely failed miners, drifters, vagrants or people just down on their luck who had escaped north to try again, mostly without success. The economic life, what there was of it, was largely in the hands of the industrious Chinese, who almost totally dominated retailing, horticulture, carting, cleaning, hairdressing, and, of course, mining.

The Commonwealth took over government of the Territory from South Australia in 1911. Just about the only things that were achieved during the period of SA's involvement were the Overland Telegraph's Station and a narrow-gauge rail line which went from Port Darwin south about 400 kilometres (eventually 500 kilometres, to Larrimah). You can still see the railway's embankments from the Stuart Highway.

East Point Beach. One of the beautiful spots that makes Darwin such a popular tourist destination

PHOTOGRAPH BY CONSERVATION COMMISSION

Otherwise Darwin, with the exception of some fine buildings such as the Administrator's Residency and the Commercial Bank (built in the late nineteenth century on the corner of Bennett and Smith streets), remained a backwater, where almost every conceivable tropical disease, including malaria and dengue fever, was rampant and where elementary amenities were absent. As one historian said of this period, the Territory remained a vast iceberg of failure in a sea of prosperity. Darwin perhaps was the tip of the iceberg as well as the best symbol of that failure.

Things did not get much better after the Commonwealth's takeover. In 1912, the Federal Government sent a Scottish veterinarian and academic of some note, John Anderson Gilruth, to administer the Territory, thereby starting a chain of events that led to Darwin's own Rum Rebellion. A well-meaning man steeped in the great traditions of the British Empire, Gilruth wanted to see this land prosper and for that he needed investment on a grand scale. He got it in the form of Vesteys Meatworks, a meat processing plant that was built in 1914/15 by the powerful British cattle baron, Lord Vestey (the owner of much of Victoria River Downs), at enormous cost on

Bullocky Point, the site of Darwin High School. But with capitalism came unionism and, in Darwin, the emergent labour movement took a peculiarly virulent nature. The Vesteys venture was plagued by strikes until it closed down in 1919, after only two haphazard killing seasons, and at a formidable loss.

On 17 December 1918, about 1000 workers assembled in front of the Administrator's Residency and demanded Gilruth's removal. Some of the workers invaded the grounds and a violent scuffle broke out. The Federal Government recalled Gilruth in February 1919, after sending a gunboat to Darwin Harbour as a protective measure.

Between the two world wars, the town developed slowly. No major landmarks, except the oil tanks on top and around the slight hills at the port, were built. The tanks were built primarily to establish Darwin as a port of supply for the Australian and British navies (at a time when both navies were changing from coal to oil). This defence build-up contributed to a slight growth in population to about 5000 civilians (Aborigines were not included in the census at this time) by 1939.

On 19 February 1942, at 9:58 am, a force of 188 Japanese planes launched a devastating attack on Darwin from the same aircraft carriers that had attacked Pearl Harbor. Two hours later, 54 land-based Japanese bombers attacked the RAAF aerodrome: 243 people died and between 300 and 400 were wounded in the attack. Also, 12 ships were sunk or put out of action in the harbour. Many houses were flattened and those that remained standing were vandalised and looted by Australian and American military personnel, who believed the Japanese were about to land and did not want to leave anything to the invaders. The bombing of Darwin (followed by more than 60 recorded bombing raids to the end of 1943) remains the worst attack on Australian soil in history. There is a viewing platform and photo exhibit near the Administrator's Residency, which illustrates the raid with chilling accuracy.

Tunnels were dug on the port hills for oil storage but were never used. One of the tunnels, below the viewing platform, has now been transformed into a museum, which houses photographs and other memorabilia from the war years. Also, at East Point, there is a military museum with

Cyclone Tracy which struck Darwin on Christmas Eve 1974 blew the old town away and killed 64 residents, injuring many more. It remains Australia's worst peace time disaster. The Federal Government seriously considered rebuilding the city in another location, but came up against the determination of the town's people who wanted their old homes back.

PHOTOGRAPH COURTESY OF R.E. FOX

An aerial view of Darwin City. The city was completely rebuilt after being levelled by Cyclone Tracy in 1974.

relics from those years. Construction of the huge 9.2 inch gun emplacements that remain today was started in May 1941, but they were finished and test-fired only in 1944 and 1945 respectively, too late to be of any use. Ironically, the guns were sold as scrap metal to the Japanese after the war.

Darwin would not recover from the war years until well into the 1960s. There were many reasons for the slow pace of recovery, the town's isolation, lack of identifiable industries and an economic base, as well as the almost total absence of amenities considered essential in other Australian urban centres. Nor was Darwin helped by the Darwin Town Plan Act implemented by the Chifley Labor Government in 1948, which did away with freehold land tenure in favour of short-term leases. The Act, called a 'monstrous shadow' by Administrator Abbott and described as the major impediment to progress by well-known Territory historian Douglas Lockwood, ensured that business could not be established in Darwin because no bank would lend money to entrepreneurs on the basis of short-term leases. The Menzies Government, which succeeded Labor in 1949, changed short-term leases for long-term leases, but did not re-establish freehold tenure. It rigidly controlled release of land with the result that there were constant shortages of housing right through the 1950s and 1960s, and what was available, was very expensive.

On 24 December 1974, when Cyclone Tracy struck, the city was still relatively undeveloped. Some have argued Darwin was little more than a sleepy tropical outpost where Commonwealth public servants did penance before transferring to the kinder climates of the south. Cyclone Tracy blew the old town away. Hurricane winds that, in some instances, reached 400 kilometres an hour, destroyed Darwin, killed 64 people, and injured many more. About 30 000 residents, out of a total population of 40 000, were evacuated in the days following the cyclone, and there was doubt Darwin would ever be reconstructed or, if it were, whether it would be in the same place.

The Darwin Reconstruction Commission was established to guide the reconstruction effort, but it was plagued by bureaucratic infighting and indecision until a former Lord Mayor of Brisbane, Clem Jones, was put in charge in mid-1975. By then, many Darwin residents had taken matters in their own hands, and despite existing restrictions, had proceeded to patch up their old homes. Slowly, a new Darwin emerged. In 1980, following self-government for the Territory in July 1978, the new NT Government did away with leasehold and reintroduced freehold. At a stroke of the pen, some 14 000 leasehold titles were transformed into freehold in Darwin alone.

The city that you see today is very much the product of the years since self-government. All the suburbs beyond Casuarina were built after the cyclone. The satellite city of Palmerston was only planned in 1980/81 and construction started in 1982. The tallest building in Darwin for some years was the T & G Building in Smith Street. It is now dwarfed by several structures and others are on the way.

The frenetic growth has been accompanied by a significant effort to 'green' the city. Arguably, no comparable city in Australia enjoys so many parks, playing fields and open spaces. Landscaping by the NT Conservation Commission and the Darwin City Council is number-one priority at present. Two artificial lakes have been built near the city centre, and one more will be constructed in the northern suburbs in 1994.

Darwin now has a popluation of around 75 000 people. The transient proportion of the population is still very high, about 30 per cent a year, but it was much higher before Cyclone Tracy.

Along with a more stable population has

come another phenomenon. Darwin is a particularly cosmopolitan and tolerant urban centre. The people include some 52 ethnic groups and nationalities, who live here in harmony. This town, which had an unlovely birth and grew along strict racial guidelines, has developed into a liberal, amiable and generous community that enjoys most of the amenities of larger cities with few of their disadvantages.

There is more. Darwin is establishing deep cultural and trading links with our Asian neighbours. Hardly a week goes by without Territory officials, business people and politicians travelling to South-East Asia or without finding their Asian counterparts in Darwin. Already, the links are beginning to pay off, and there can be little doubt this city's future is inextricably woven with the future of its northern neighbours, perhaps more so than with the 'south'.

So there you have it. An, in part, unsavoury but thoroughly romantic history mixed with an enormously exciting present. I think Darwin is Australia's best-kept secret.

*M*ulti-coloured lillies festoon the Mary River floodplains, inundated by water brought by the annual monsoon.

PHOTOGRAPH BY TOM VIGUS

MARY RIVER

think that the Mary River wetlands are at least equal to those of the Magella Plains in Kakadu, and the fishing is also better than in Kakadu.

There, I've said it, rank heresy. How can anything compare with the Top End's crown jewel? Kakadu is in a class of its own—incomparable, majestic, splendid and contemptuous of lesser beings.

Well, perhaps. But I still prefer the Mary River wetlands. Let's not call them wetlands. They are really floodplains: huge, vast expanses of flooded land where waterfowl of all kinds abound. This is not a continuous river such as you find elsewhere. The Mary River is really a series of billabongs and lagoons, which are linked during the Wet season to flood the surrounding floodplains.

This is where the yearly monsoon comes home to rest. It is the home the monsoon looks for, having abandoned the Ganges Delta, soaked Malaysia, and saturated the forests of Cambodia and Indonesia. The monsoon traverses the Timor Sea to the thirsty shores of Northern Australia which welcomes the dark clouds that herald the rains. They come ponderously, preceded by the regal paraphernalia of dramatic thunder and lightning, and they make a display before discharging titanic amounts of water that will settle in these wetlands.

The water flushes out unwanted flotsam accumulated through the Dry months and gives life to barramundi and other fish. Estuarine crocodiles, stranded in the same place for some months, are now free to travel. Magpie geese squawk contentedly.

All the Mary River channels and billabongs are replenished, and nearby, the mysterious Wildman forest gets yet another reprieve, having survived for thousands of years. The striking granite outcrops of the Mount Bundy hills, the river's sentinels, are an impressive sight silhouetted by lightning against a leaden sky. Brooding and ancient, they provide an impressive backdrop to the area.

So do the waterlilies at Couzens Lookout. They contemplate the hard spatter of rain on the surface while they preen themselves under the baleful look of an old crocodile.

The scene is one of unadulterated magic. Someone in heaven waves a hand and the new rains have brought the yearly miracle yet again. The floodplains are alive and they want you to know it.

They are not jealous of Kakadu. In fact, this region hopes it will never be discovered. It is perfectly satisfied with its relative anonymity. Already, of course, the locals flock here rather than further east to its famous cousin, because they know this place's sorcery and are captivated by it. But the majority of tourists have so far passed the Mary River by. The situation may not last.

For a start, the area is much closer to

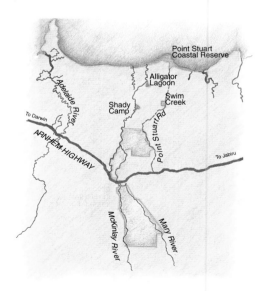

Corroboree Creek, one of the Mary River tributaries, about 185 kilometres from Darwin and a popular fishing and recreational spot for Top Enders.

PHOTOGRAPH BY TOM VIGUS

Darwin than Kakadu. The Mary River is about 185 kilometres from Darwin. It includes the Wildman Reserve, which is mentioned later in this section, the Delta Block, the Mary River Crossing Conservation Reserve, Point Stuart Reserve, Shady Camp, Stuart's Tree Historical Reserve, Swim Creek and the McKinlay River Block. Together, they form a splendid kaleidoscope of beauty, where wildlife, scenery and the sheer pleasure of wide open spaces combine. But there is more.

History, for example. Swim Creek and Shady Camp were named by the explorer John McDouall Stuart at the end of his epic walk across Australia. Swim Creek was so named because Stuart is supposed to have swum here to shake off the stifling heat of the coastal plains. And he named Shady Camp for the generous shade offered by trees that have long vanished, grazed out by buffalo. Only a few scrawny fig trees remain.

There used to be thousands of buffalo here, but they were shot during the Brucellosis and Tuberculosis Eradication Campaign (BTEC). With them disappeared a legend of the coastal plains—the buffalo shooters whose names you will find in landmarks (and watermarks) stretching from here to Arnhem Land. The Hardys, the Coopers, Cahills and Coles—truly rugged individuals who pioneered this land on horseback long before anyone thought a road could be built to the area all the way from Port Darwin.

A report by the NT Conservation Commission gives a fair account of the flora and fauna of this area. The tall grasses and sedges of the floodplain, the tropical woodland, the monsoon rainforests and the paperbark swamps support huge numbers of mammals, including agile wallabies and antilopine wallaroos, native rats, bandicoots, possums and sugar gliders. There are also red-cheeked dunnarts, black and little red flying foxes and numerous bats. The tiniest marsupial in the Top End, the common planigale, lives here in the woodland. Dingoes are common, and so are wild pigs. If you are interested in wildlife, this is the place to see it.

Hundreds of bird species have been recorded and reptiles abound—saltwater crocodiles and many types of snakes, including the deadly king brown and black whip, as well as a variety of large pythons and goannas.

Special note should be made of the magpie geese, which were once common throughout Australia. These wetlands now provide one of the last refuges of this species, with the Mary River being the main breeding and rearing area.

The flora is equally striking. The open forest is dominated by eucalypts, although you will find plenty of turkey bush, fern-leaved grevillea (which tiny birds love because of its sweet flower) and common fan palms.

The extensive floodplain system is fringed by natural springs, which support dense stands of monsoon rainforest. Where you find wild nutmeg, banyan, cluster figs and carpent-aria palms. In the boundaries are carpentaria palms, leichhardt trees and freshwater mangroves. A tiny caterpillar on the fresh-water mangrove leaves can give a painful rash, so stay away from it. Paperbark swamps in this area are usually dominated by the broad-leaved melaleuca.

These coastal flooplains were formed at the end of the last Ice Age, maybe 10 000 years ago, when rising sea levels drowned river mouths and coastal river valleys. Old sand dunes (cheniers) around Point Stuart and north of Lake Finnis prevented saltwater intrusion of the freshwater wetlands. But, in some areas, dunes were broken down either by buffalo or, it is believed, were blasted by fishermen to allow boat access to the sea. Salt water then penetrated far inland, killing thousands of hectares of paperbarks. The artificial barrage at Shady Camp is one of the many blocks in the system that have been successful in keeping the salt water from penetrating any further.

Shady Camp is located at the meeting place between fresh and salt water on the Mary River. A causeway has been built over a natural rockbar to stop the salt water from coming in. Downstream from the causeway, Sampan Creek is one of the two tidal channels that drain the Mary River system into the sea.

This casual meeting of fresh and salt water produces the most spectacular barramundi fishing in Northern Australia. Here, the mullet converge to feed on algae washed down by the fresh water at the end of the Wet. Greedy barramundi and other fish follow to feed on the mullet.

And, of course, the crocodile is never too far away when there is plenty of fish. This is the ideal habitat for estuarine crocodiles. They can be seen here as they can be seen

nowhere else in the world, and the best time for that is the Dry, when it is much cooler and the lazy creatures soak up the sun on the river banks, staring impassively as the fishing boats cruise slowly past.

The Mary River region is a hidden pearl in the Top End. It has not been developed with the tourist in mind, at least not yet, but the locals have been coming here for many years to fish, camp out for the weekend, or simply for a scenic drive.

This very attractive area includes unequalled wildlife, scenery and some of the best fishing in Northern Australia. It is relatively untouched, but I don't imagine this will last. It is close to Darwin, readily accessible during the cool months of the year, when most visitors come, and crisscrossed by good dirt tracks. Conventional vehicles can reach most areas during the Dry, but flooding in the Wet causes indefinite road closures.

Facilities are getting better. Overnight accommodation can be found at such places as Point Stuart Wilderness Lodge, Corroboree Park Tavern, the Bark Hut Inn and the Wimray Safari Lodge.

All this means that the NT Conservation Commission has a job on its hands, because some parts of the Mary River floodplains and region, particularly breeding areas for birdlife and other animals, should be assiduously protected from excessive visitation.

Steps have already been taken to ensure this. But if you intend visiting this extraordinary area, please take care of it. Leave pets at home and bring back rubbish. Also, keep an eye on those crocodiles.

An airboat glides over the marvellous floodplains of the Mary River in the Top End.

PHOTOGRAPH BY TOM VIGUS/CCNT

Barramundi fishing at Shady Camp can be truly rewarding: just ask the local fishermen.

PHOTOGRAPH BY ALEX JULIUS

WILDMAN RIVER

Wildman River Station is the site of the Conservation Commission's Wildman Reserve. It came as a complete surprise to me.

I expected a couple of scenic places surrounded by uninteresting buffalo country or more of the same old savannah–eucalypt that distinguishes much of the Top End.

Instead I discovered a delightful park with almost unlimited possibilities. Wildman of course is adjacent to Kakadu and is readily accessible from Darwin by conventional vehicles. The wet season however does bring flooding to lowland streams and access to the park may be restricted. The most comfortable time to visit is during the dry season between May and October.

There are really two aspects to the park. One is its discovered potential. The other is undiscovered … but not for long.

Well known are the vast billabongs discharging into the Mary River. They are home to millions of birds — particularly magpie geese — huge saltwater crocodiles and expanses of incredibly delicate waterlilies.

The ranger in charge, Simon Oster, took me for a leisurely cruise by dinghy and outboard motor through the Wildman Lagoon, a stretch of clear water fringed by blankets of blue, red and white lilies. The colour names are humdrum and pedestrian. Blue, red and white are not adequate descriptions for hues and shades altogether too subtle and deft to put in simple words.

The lilies in comfortable beds of broad green leaves on which little birds, lily trotters, hop gracefully in search of food. As we were cruising along, the brown shape of a large saltwater crocodile broke the sedate waters, swimming lazily towards the opposite shore. It added to a rare splendour, an intangible feeling that here at least all was well with the world.

Simon, only half jokingly, said to me: 'Be kind to us. Don't make it appear too wonderful.'

His fear, shared by other rangers elsewhere, is that after the park's potential is discovered there will be an invasion by visitors and that this will detract from the park's pristine beauty.

Well, the invasion is inevitable. I answered that I would probably fail to do the park justice because the scenery has to be felt and seen—it cannot be adequately described.

I recommend Couzens Lookout for one of the most extraordinary sights on earth. Literally as far as the eye can see, dark blue waters festooned by gently bobbing lilies. Beyond are the flatlands of the Mary River basin broken only by clumps of paperbark forest. Immediately in front, a crop of brown rocks jutting into the huge lagoon. In between, water and flowers. Above, the blue sky with the sun caressing everything.

Not far from Couzens Lookout is another sightseeing platform, North Rockhole.

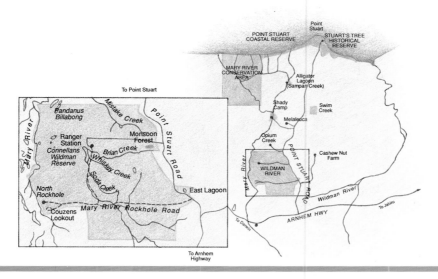

Couzens Lookout takes its name from a long serving and dedicated Territory ranger, the late Ken Couzens, who spent several years at Wildman Reserve. The view of the wide expanses of the Mary River floodplains from Couzens Lookout is breath-taking.

PHOTOGRAPH BY DAVID SILVA

51

PHOTOGRAPH BY FRANK WOERLE

The Mary River wetlands are home to an amazing array of birdlife. This magpie goose hatchling is but one of the several species. The region is known as one of the most important breeding areas for magpie geese in the Territory.

The Rockhole consists of a pile of large granite slabs intruding a fair way into the water. Nature's arrangement has fashioned it into a perfect jetty or a vantage point to soak in the marvellous beauty of the place or view the antics of an occasional crocodile as it sunbakes or searches for food.

There are camping grounds and a boat ramp at North Rockhole providing access to the channels of the Mary River.

This is also a site of significance for local Aborigines who, in times past, used the rocks to crush nardoo or grass seeds for paste. This is one of the few semi-sedentary activities Aborigines developed in their otherwise hunting and gathering history. The worn cavities on the rocks are still clearly visible. As well there are some old Aboriginal living sites in the area that should be of interest to visitors wishing to broaden their knowledge of the original inhabitants of this fascinating region.

Almost certainly one of the principal reasons for Aboriginal predilection for the area was that the fishing in this particular billabong and neighbouring watercourses rates as among the best in the Top End.

While on this subject I must mention a few things about crocodiles which abound in these waters. There are only two kinds in Australia. They are the saltwater, or estuarine crocodile, and the freshwater or Johnston's crocodile. The first *(Crocodylus porosus)*, often referred to as 'salties', are maneaters. The second *(Crocodylus johnstoni),* normally known as 'freshies', are not considered dangerous but should nevertheless be treated with caution.

Male salties mature at three to four metres and about sixteen years of age, females at two to three metres and ten years of age. Freshies, found only in Australia, are considerably smaller and usually quite timid. They are distinguished by their snout, narrow and long for the freshies and broad and fierce for the salties. Both are protected animals, a policy resented by some Top Enders who fear they are multiplying beyond control and pose a threat to human life. In reality there have been very few fatalities.

Nevertheless, you should take care with salties— a misnomer for the species since they can be found in many freshwater streams, swamps and billabongs as well as in the sea. The best protection against salties is a very simple one: do not swim or bathe in waters where the Conservation Commission has signs indicating that saltwater crocodiles inhabit the area. That most certainly applies to the Wildman River region where crocodiles, incidentally the

PHOTOGRAPH BY DAVID SILVA

enior Ranger, Dave West, discusses the wetland environment with Major Les Hiddins.

PHOTOGRAPH BY FRANK WOERLE

ily leaves make ideal platforms for insect-catching frogs.

A saltwater crocodile: this fine specimen was estimated at six metres.

PHOTOGRAPH BY TONY FORDE

largest living reptiles since dinosaurs roamed the earth millions of years ago, are everywhere. By all means enjoy them cruising in all their glory. But do not take risks.

On the way back to the ranger station Simon drove through endless floodplains now almost free of buffalo. He was quite emphatic: 'We must rid the park of buffaloes and feral pigs,' he said, pointing out the enormous damage caused to the plains and surrounding countryside by the two animals.

The damage was obvious. The ground, cracked and churned through the impact of countless hooves and rooting snouts, is only now in the process of a slow recovery. When it does finally recover the flatlands will add yet another dimension to the immense beauty of Wildman.

But there were other surprises in this delightful park that have not yet been discovered. One is a sizeable area of the most incredible rainforest. A marvellous hideaway uncannily replete with the familiar sounds of the jungle and cool even under the broiling midday sun.

The forest, named Brian Creek Monsoonal Forest, is easily accessible and situated only a couple of kilometres from the main ranger station access road.

It is a perfect place to relax, have a picnic or take a long walk through a world that was once common throughout northern Australia but is now only rarely found in small pockets here and there.

The Commission has preliminary plans for walkways that will take visitors to the top of the trees for bird watching and photography. It should be an unforgettable experience.

Enough to satiate the senses? Not quite. A short drive away is Shady Camp, one of the Top End's best known barramundi fishing spots. The site is not scenic like so many others in this unusual park, but it is a must for keen fishermen. People wishing to add some 'barra' fillets to their evening barbecues or just enjoy crocodile watching and photography will appreciate Shady Camp.

Nearby is another marvellous waterhole,

the East Lagoon Billabong, with excellent wet season waterfowl observation vantage points, marvellous for photography.

East Lagoon is on the way to Point Stuart, some 40 kilometres to the north on dirt tracks. The area has not yet been opened up for tourism but, hopefully, it will shortly. The remarkable variety of flora and fauna, including a true haven for wallabies, makes the drive well worthwhile. And at the end there is the Point itself.

I stood on the precise spot the explorer, John McDouall Stuart had stood after his epic 1862 south–north crossing of Australia and tried to understand how he had felt. This was in fact his sixth expedition to the interior and he had finally succeeded where Burke and Wills had tragically failed, their bones bleached by the desert sun.

Stuart, a man with a well-developed taste for a strong drink, probably looked at the vast ocean in front of his eyes and let the sight wash away years of harsh struggle and frustration. He stood on the wild mangrove-fringed beach littered with clean debris and, undoubtedly summoning the full strength of his pride, he allowed himself a few moments of reflection.

For Stuart knew that he had walked not just through one of the most inhospitable and hostile regions on earth, but into the pages of history. By the time he returned to Adelaide he was no more than a walking skeleton but, perhaps, it did not matter any more. What mattered was the eternal vision of the open spaces and the stars that he would carry with him for the short time he still had to live.

Nothing has changed since Stuart stepped into this hidden corner of the northern shore. The rough white sands speckled by a myriad tiny shells, the twisted remains of dead trees brought to the shore by angry seas, the soft murmur of the surf and the incredibly bright stars in a night that goes on and on.

The whole play of ecology, including exceptional flora and fauna, are all there for visitors to come and see ... and perhaps even allow themselves to feel just as Stuart had felt. Wildman is a treasure just waiting to be discovered.

The wonders of Kakadu. Intriguing escarpment formations of the East Alligator region.

PHOTOGRAPH BY FRANK WOERLE

56

KAKADU NATIONAL PARK

*T*he Kakadu National Park, approximately 250 kilometres from Darwin on a good road, is in a class of its own. The park has been popularised by *Crocodile Dundee,* but the films do not really do it justice.

For Kakadu is a brutal, savage park. The rivers and billabongs are unswimmable because large saltwater crocodiles are everywhere. The murky dark waters of the floodplains contain danger.

The imposing escarpment is the home of unspeakable spirits. The gnarled rock formations are the work of a devil. Angry gorges spewing sheer white foam have not been shaped for the enjoyment or wonder of mere mortals. They exist to frighten and awe.

The massive park is a piece of ground wrenched in fury from mother earth and flung against the crust where it remains as a twisted and contorted mockery of the laws of nature.

Kakadu has no right to be. It is an affront to the senses and a contradiction of the neat rules that govern the world. The beauty and the beast live here.

And that is what makes Kakadu so intensely attractive. For if the park were just another easy promenade through manicured gardens it would still be wonderful but it would lack attraction. That comes from Kakadu's ineffable combination of majesty and grandeur, of ugliness and grace.

This is of course very much a personal viewpoint. A more objective view would see Kakadu as an ancient sandstone mesa or plateau averaging 250–300 metres elevation. This is the famed Kakadu escarpment and its governing feature. It winds for more than 1000 kilometres from Murgenella in the north to the Katherine Gorge in the south. This is the catchment area for the South Alligator, the East Alligator, the Katherine, the Roper and the Daly rivers. The water, angry during the monsoonal season, has cut through the hard limestone rocks carving spectacular gorges.

Above all, however, the escarpment lords over the park and oversees the lowlands and its unbelievable flora and fauna.

The black soil plains of the floodlands are the home of lagoons full of waterlilies and fringed by majestic pandanus, paperbarks,

△ Camping

The lotus bird or cone-crested jacana makes for truly interesting observation as it crosses swamps, stepping from lily pad to lily pad.

PHOTOGRAPH BY FRANK WOERLE

A magnificent black-necked stork in flight. Commonly known as a jabiru, it is Australia's only native stork.

wild hibiscus, gardenia and grevillea. The ubiquitous eucalypt and cycads are everywhere as well, creating a riotous ambience of colour and monotony, of sameness and variety.

As is the case with the rest of the Top End, Kakadu was once covered by tropical jungle. Little remains except in some hidden gorges and sheltered corners where *Livistona* and carpentaria palms grow, providing welcome shade for mosses, ferns and, sometimes, incredibly delicate orchids.

For this is a landscape more than 2000 million years old, the product of massive sedimentation and weathering. It has survived countless ice ages and greenhouse effects and, without doubt, will survive countless more.

The immense lowlands become flooded during the Wet and thousands upon thousands of birds come here to nest and procreate. About 275 species have been identified.

And the unique environment has also spawned more than 1000 kinds of plants, 50 mammals, 75 reptiles, 25 frogs and 55 species of fish. Many are rare and occur nowhere else, and species new to science continue to be discovered in this vast natural retreat.

Nor can any mention of Kakadu escape the original inhabitants, the Aborigines. Indeed the very name, Kakadu, is just another way of saying Gagadju, one of the main language groups in the area.

Science is confused as to the exact date of human habitation in Kakadu. Some put it at 23 000 years, others a great deal longer. It would not be at all surprising, as archaeology and the study of prehistory advances, to discover that humans have been in this area for at least 100 000 years. Certainly the rock art at Kakadu is by far the most significant example of prehistoric art in the world. The Obiri Rock, easy driving from Jabiru, is probably the best known art site but not the best Kakadu offers.

The Deaf Adder Gorge is more substantial. Nevertheless, Obiri has a great deal to offer including magnificent views of the Magella

*T*he frill neck
lizard, easily
identifiable by its
large neck frill
which it raises in
defence when
threatened.

PHOTOGRAPH BY FRANK WOERLE

floodplains west of Oenpelli. Another overhanging gallery at Hawk Dreaming, near Cannon Hill, has paintings older than Obiri's. Nourlangie Rock and Sawcut Gorge are also the sites of splendid rock art.

The Aborigines here must have come close to a transition from nomadic hunting and gathering to sedentary habits. Here civilisation 23 000 years ago was arguably the most advanced on earth. Not only had Aboriginal clans developed a very high form of rock art (the famed Altamira cave paintings in Spain, for example, date only about 13 000 years) but they were using stone tools such as stone axes and grinding rocks. They had also developed highly advanced rituals that governed their lives from birth to death. Many remain, making Kakadu an absorbing region for anthropologists and archaeologists.

It should be noted here that some of the art sites mentioned are out of bounds to visitors because of their special significance to the Aboriginal traditional owners of Kakadu.

The park's complex geography has spilled over into politics. In 1978 the Aboriginal traditional owners decided to transfer control of Kakadu from the Northern Territory Government to the Federal Government. The Canberra-based Australian National Parks and Wildlife Service (ANPWS), not the Conservation Commission of the Northern Territory (CCNT), manages the park. The issue is still hotly debated with the NT Government desiring control of Kakadu.

Economics has also intruded into the demands of ecology and the environment, for Kakadu contains the largest proven uranium deposits in the world. Ranger uranium mine, on a slice of excised land in Kakadu, has been operating for some years. Two others, Koongarra and Jabiluka, are likely to come on stream at some time in the future.

Kakadu is therefore much more than a park. It is a bruising, hurting ground where Aboriginal history and folklore, the Dreamtime, and the bustling, aggressive advance of Western industrial society have clashed over a ferocious landscape. If you miss that you have missed the real significance of Kakadu.

Tourists prefer to visit Kakadu during the cooler dry months. This is understandable because the climate does get rather oppressive in the build-up months of November and December and during the ensuing monsoonal rains. In my view, however, Kakadu is at its best during the Wet. That is when the park really comes alive.

By the end of the dry season some of Kakadu's most spectacular waterfalls, Jim Jim and Twin Falls for example, are dry. The rock formations are still worth the trip but the spouting, foaming torrent of water that makes the falls such a wonderful spectacle is often missing.

The sad picture is compounded by the fact that the tracks to Jim Jim and Twin Falls are both inaccessible during the best viewing season, the Wet.

The falls most likely to have substantial flow is UDP Falls, well in the south of the main park area. The area was used for the filming of Crocodile Dundee and will be familiar to the millions of people around the world who enjoyed the film.

You can visit UDP by travelling down the Kakadu Highway from Jabiru to the gold mining town of Pine Creek. The road will take you to Yellow Waters, a beguiling waterway where crocodiles can be watched at leisure from one of the motor launches cruising the still, dark waters.

Two other singularly beautiful sites, Goose Camp and Red Lily Lagoon, which have been closed for some years, are now open to visitors through the services of an Aboriginal-owned tourist organisation.

Finally, it must be said, the controversial nature of the park includes uranium mining which some people have been led to believe robs the park of much of its value. This is quite simply not correct. Take a helicopter trip and you may be amazed to discover that Ranger hardly rates a pinprick in the savage immensity of Kakadu.

So there you have it, Kakadu, warts and all. An impressive park which, unfortunately, is not yet developed to anywhere near its full potential.

*A*boriginal rock paintings, *Deaf Adder Gorge, Kakadu National Park.*

PHOTOGRAPH BY FRANK WOERLE

*T*win Falls at the height of the wet season. The view from a helicopter or light plane is truly spectacular where the river falls hundreds of metres to continue on its way.

PHOTOGRAPH BY FRANK WOERLE

Some springs at the base of the escarpment flow all year round, attracting a wide variety of wildlife during the dry season.

PHOTOGRAPH BY FRANK WOERLE

ern leafed grevillea (Grevillea pteridifolia) *grows in the sandstone rock country of Kakadu.*

PHOTOGRAPH BY FRANK WOERLE

It remains to be seen whether common sense will prevail in the future. That surely must lie in a proper balance between conservation and development.

Kakadu's managers are saddled with the worst of two worlds. They have not developed an infrastructure that will allow them reasonable control over the many thousands of visitors that flock to the park.

And they have failed to discourage visitation.

Perhaps it would be more intelligent to accept the facts, that is, people from all over the world will continue to be attracted, almost hypnotically so, by Kakadu's undeniable grandeur and will want to see it with their own eyes.

Perennial water supplies are the lifeblood of isolated rainforest pockets.

PHOTOGRAPH BY DAVID SILVA

68

LITCHFIELD PARK

itchfield Park, about two hours' easy driving from Darwin, is a delight. It has something for everyone. Great swimming in crystal clear waters, bushwalking, some difficult tracks for four-wheel drive enthusiasts, magnificent scenery and top camping.

It is rapidly being discovered by more and more visitors who find the park just the place to relax beside large pools formed by cascading waters or, if they are so inclined, engage in some scenic bushwalking through rugged bushland.

Until recently access was difficult requiring four-wheel drive vehicles and a well developed sense of adventure. But a formed gravel road providing dry weather two-wheel drive access from Batchelor and the Wangi Road have made it a great deal easier for the average visitor to enjoy Litchfield.

The road constitutes a magnificent scenic drive providing access to two great camping spots: Wangi Falls and Florence Falls. The rest, and arguably the best of the park, still demands effort beyond that provided by a conventional car.

Wangi Falls is a favourite with families or groups for a weekend outing. It features a large natural pool formed by a tall waterfall cascading gracefully from red cliffs. There is a gently sloping sandy beach-head fringed by trees and fresh lawns. The pool, more like a small lake, is bound by rainforest with tall thin carpentaria palms featuring prominently as they search for the sun above the canopy.

A late evening or night swim to the walled end of the waterfall is a marvellous experience. Only the stars, unbelievably bright and close, and the gossamer pale stream of water falling from way above are visible. The rest is impenetrably dark.

A slippery hold on the rocks just below the sprinkle of heavy drops provides an opportunity to stop and think. Here there is only one's self and the night broken by shafts of translucent silver. Beyond is darkness. Between are the odd bird cries and the occasional gust of lazy breeze against luxuriant fronds.

Then a slow swim back to the tiny beach and a walk to the camp, about 200 metres away.

Firewood burning, a steak sizzling on a hotplate, red wine and cold beer followed by long talks about nothing before adjourning to the tent or simply a sleeping bag for a good night's sleep. Just make sure you have a mosquito net or some other kind of protection against insects.

Another swim before breakfast, cool waters invigorating and refreshing. Then the real Litchfield adventure begins.

For the park is above all an exciting adventure. By all means enjoy Wangi Falls and its twin, Florence Falls. They are both wonderful and relaxing. But if you want a truly unforgettable experience follow your visit to those two falls with several other options.

First visit Tolmer Falls, then go to the Lost City. Try also to sandwich the Sandy Creek lagoon and waterfall nestled among some of

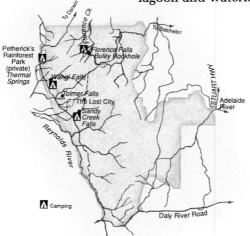

Brightly coloured fungal growth appears in moister areas during the wet season.

the most remarkable flora in the park.

All demand the use of four-wheel drive vehicles or (my favourite) bushwalking.

Tolmer Falls is a place of incomparable beauty. One almost feels there is something sinister about such a peaceful paradise. The approach to the falls and lagoon is unexceptional. It consists largely of open wooded savannah country similar to most of the Top End. Then, rounding up a hillock, there it is. A patch of rainforest populated by flora that should have disappeared with the great reptiles of the Mesozoic but, for some unexplained reason, did not.

The walk through the forest to the lagoon is in fact a fantastic passage into another world and another geography. The stream in the middle provides the background for one of the most exotic collection of plants and birds on earth. I was told by a Conservation Commission ranger, Tom Nicholls, that many of the plants had not even been classified yet. The statement is not difficult to believe. There is such a luxuriant proliferation of flora that it, quite literally, defies description.

The walk itself is well worth the

reasonably easy four-wheel drive trip to Tolmer, but of course there is more, much more. The lagoon is the most strikingly beautiful in the Territory. Set in a magnificent amphitheatre of imposing red cliffs, it features an ample cave where hundreds of bats make their home. And at one end of the cave there is a wonderful pool of thermal waters bubbling happily away, just waiting for tired bodies.

Tolmer Falls deserves to be classified as the jewel in Litchfield's crown. I was told by the ranger in charge, Peter Egan, that there will be a road for conventional vehicle access to Tolmer. A suspension bridge is planned within the rainforested gorge, below the rim of the waterfall but above the treetops. This means visitors can actually see the scenery below without the need to trample all over it. Sounds like an excellent idea.

Nor is this the end of Litchfield. A couple of hours walking distance from Tolmer, or less through a longer and difficult four-wheel drive track, there is the Lost City.

The City is a natural geological formation, but you don't have to believe this rather prosaic explanation. For the perfectly

$\mathcal{W}$*ith its trunk scarred from recent bushfires, the cycad bursts forth with lush new fronds. It is considered one of the oldest types of plants existing today.*

PHOTOGRAPH BY DAVID SILVA

71

*L*ush vegetation surrounds the inviting waters of Litchfield Park's Tolmer Falls.

PHOTOGRAPH BY TONY FORDE

73

*T*he weathered
and eroded
formations of
Litchfield Park's
Lost City are a
photographer's
delight.

PHOTOGRAPH BY TONY FORDE

shaped walls, narrow doors, huge gates and massive domes are of such consummate workmanship that it is hard to believe there was no human intervention in their building.

Sunsets against the solid fortress should not be missed. And later in the evening, when only the stars break the darkness, light a small fire and watch the flickering flames throw strange shadows on the walls and gates built by a forgotten race of giants. And feel at one with time and an era that will never return.

Only a short distance south of the Lost City is another marvellous place—Sandy Creek Falls. It is accessible by four-wheel drive vehicles only, but if you really want to explore the incredible flora here you would be better advised to do it on foot.

The best way is by following a track along the western escarpment of the Park from Petherick's Rainforest Park through Sandy Creek. The escarpment contains many delightful cascades and small waterfalls, and associated with these perennial wet areas are small pockets of rainforest. The Conservation Commission also intends to establish horse trails. Where appropriate tethering sites are established, the horse rider will be able to visit otherwise inaccessible sensitive scenic attractions.

Also, you should not miss the Blyth Homestead. Established in 1924, it probably arose out of the Commonwealth's moves to open up more pastoral land in the north. Apart from some tin mining at Mt Tolmer (near the falls of the same name), little had happened during the long years of South Australian administration of the Territory (1863—1911). The homestead's name comes from the pastoral block referred to as the Hundred of Blyth. It is well preserved as a relic of harder times and worth a visit by those interested in history.

The Conservation Commission has now concluded a thoughtful draft management plan for Litchfield which includes an expansion of recreational and tourism attractions in the Park.

Among them are Ada Creek, Woodland Campground, Tabletop Swamp, the Western Escarpment, Walker Creek and Bamboo Creek Tin Mine. They are all bewitching places, each with their own individual appeal as if they wanted to compete for the affection of nature lovers.

It is not at all difficult to fall in love with them. Ada Creek consists of a series of scenic waterfalls and plunge pools formed by a small cascade at the headwaters. Woodland Forest is a very large thickly wooded flat area where it is always cool and full of enticing shadows. Here you can easily forget that man, the primate, has moved ahead into the age of computers and global communications. Those mature trees and their splendid foliage are made to soothe the mind and wash the spirit.

Tabletop Swamp is small but exquisite, do not feel cheated by the size because this water reservoir in fact provides the flow for all the major attractions of the Park. It is located about 5 kilometres north-east of the Tolmer Falls turnoff, and is surrounded by paperbark forest which is home for a marvellous variety of wildlife.

The Western Escarpment is nowhere near as imposing as, say, the Kakadu Escarpment but it is interesting in itself mainly because of the series of small waterfalls and monsoon forest patches along its whole length. It is ready made for bushwalkers who enjoy losing themselves in an almost untouched wilderness.

Walker Creek headwaters include a series of attractive little gorges and sandstone outcrops which begin in an astonishingly beautiful palm-fringed upstream spring. The Bamboo Creek Tin Mine was closed only 25 years ago and the old structures and rusting machinery speak of history. The place is therefore a relic and valuable just for that. But it also happens to be very attractive with creeks and monsoon forest vegetation.

Treat Litchfield Park as you would a precious heirloom because that is what it is, a valuable possession that must be passed on to generations.

The spectacular Katherine Gorge, carved through time by the seasonally flooding waters of the Katherine River. Katherine Gorge consists of not one but a series of thirteen gorges, not all of which are accessible throughout the year, due to the rising and falling of the water level of the Katherine River.

PHOTOGRAPH BY FRANK WOERLE

76

AROUND & WEST OF KATHERINE

*T*hey called it the Land of the Never Never, a land so harsh in a climate so oppressive that European man could never survive.

But the pioneers who struck north from the security of the big cities against tremendous odds did survive. Cattle thrived and multiplied, vegetables and fruit grew well near rivers and streams, and at Pine Creek fortunes were won and lost on the goldfields.

As a backdrop to those pioneering struggles, nature excelled herself. The thirteen breathtaking gorges on the Katherine River, now protected for all Australians as Nitmiluk National Park, provide a boat ride into prehistory. The Cutta Cutta Caves are home to a unique species of bat, thermal springs boil to the surface at Mataranka and, further west, the wildly beautiful and mostly unexplored country of the Keep River and Gregory National Parks are a fitting introduction to the Northern Territory from Western Australia.

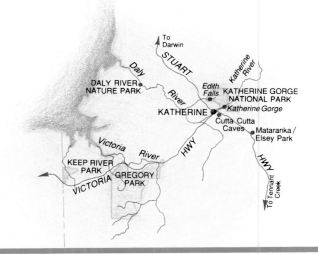

L ong and shortneck turtles occur in all freshwater streams and waterholes in the Top End and are an important food source for Aboriginal people.

PHOTOGRAPH BY FRANK WOERLE

KATHERINE GORGE

(NITMILUK NATIONAL PARK)

Katherine Gorge needs no introduction. It is one of the most visited and well recognised Territory parks. Just 32 kilometres from the Katherine township, entrance is via a sealed road through some fairly drab and uninteresting countryside which certainly does not prepare the visitor for the marvels of the gorge.

Katherine Gorge Park, now known by its Jawoyn name of Nitmiluk National Park, is not just one gorge, but 13 splendid gorges offering not only a scenic wonder but facilities for a variety of recreational activities such as canoeing, swimming, picnics, bushwalking and photography. Or you can simply sit back and relax while a boat takes you for a cruise between the towering cliffs.

The whole experience is a fantastic trip into rare geology or perhaps into the world's earliest history. For Katherine Gorge began to be formed some 1400 to 1800 million years ago in the Pre-Cambrian period. This means that the rocks there were shaped before life appeared on earth. These rocks have been made wise by the passing of earth's epic history. They have witnessed the first abundant forms of life develop around them. They have been covered by thick rainforest and have been washed by the passing of eons. Great reptiles rested here or lay in ambush waiting for prey. Of them, only freshwater

crocodiles remain. Long, long before Man came, these red cliffs had grown old and had learned great wisdom.

So the story about Katherine Gorge cannot be confined just to the magnificent scenery or to leisure activities in this truly great park. It must include the epic history of nature, the shaping of bountiful and generous mother earth.

The flora within the park is nothing less than striking. Some 450 species have been recorded including at least six considered endangered.

There are also 168 species of birds including darters, little pied cormorants and little black cormorants.

As well some 39 species of fish, including barramundi and freshwater long tom, are to be found in the gorge's perennial waters.

Tortoises, sand goannas and water monitors join freshwater crocodiles (but no salties) in the Katherine Gorge.

Although the Katherine River was first discovered by the European explorer Ludwig Leichhardt in 1844, it was named by the South Australian, John McDouall Stuart, on 4 July 1862, after Catherine, the daughter of his patron, James Chambers.

It is not known who was the first European to see the gorge. It could not have been Stuart because he crossed the river some 80 kilometres upstream from Katherine itself. Leichhardt, with his insatiable curiosity, may well have caught a

The brilliant colour of the bloodwood flower.

The native water hyacinth adds a beautiful array of colour to the waterways.

*L*eea rubra, *a favourite bush tucker.*

*W*ild apples (Syzigium suborbiculare).

PHOTOGRAPHS BY FRANK WOERLE

glimpse of the powerful gorge, but he left no traces or record. Another explorer, David Lindsay, followed the river down in 1883 until the terrain became altogether too rugged and hostile forcing him to cut across country to the familiar landmark of the Overland Telegraph. If this record is accurate, Lindsay would have come very close, within five or six kilometres, to the first and second gorges. After him there were cattlemen, missionaries and traders, but no single outstanding personality to whom the discovery can be credited, although it is widely believed that Alfred Giles, the manager of Springvale Station and a very experienced bushman, was the first European to sight the first entrance.

The facilities at Katherine Gorge are very good. They include a Visitor Centre, picnic and barbecue areas, toilets and a public boat ramp where, according to information provided by the Conservation Commission, boats up to four metres and with motors up to eight kilowatts (10 h.p.) may be launched.

Also, private businesses operate a camping ground, kiosk and boat tours. The camping ground has ablutions blocks and sites (with and without power) for tents, caravans and coaches. Groceries, film, souvenirs and petrol are available.

And that is what makes the park such a success. Tourists come in droves because they know they can enjoy the stunning scenery in comfort and can also, if they wish, engage in adventurous pursuits such as canoeing or bushwalking without too many restrictions and in safety.

Canoeing through the gorge is unforgettable but won't take you to some of the astonishingly beautiful areas in the 180 000 hectare park that bushwalking will.

Crystal Falls, about 25 kilometres north of the gorge itself, while not as spectacular, is more beautiful. As its name indicates, Crystal Falls consists of a 30 metre high crystal clear waterfall fully enclosed by rainforest.

It takes about one and a half days of walking to get there. The track, marked with white posts, leads first to Biddlecombe

Cascades where, as well as a good creek and rockhole escarpment, there are some striking Aboriginal rock arrangements.

The best time of the year for the walk, which extends from Crystal Falls to 17 Mile Falls and finally to Edith Falls 76 kilometres away, is from April to the end of September when sunny days and cool nights prevail.

Bushwalkers should wear sturdy shoes and a broad-brimmed hat as protection against the sun. Take plenty of water as well although Biddlecombe and Crystal carry good water even in the driest of dry seasons.

This walking track, particularly if followed all the way to Edith, needs a map which can be obtained from the Lands Department in the Territory. The markers on the Edith Falls track stop after crossing the wetlands near the Edith River on the 55 kilometre mark. The next 20 kilometres are best negotiated by stepping across the river to the drier western side and just following it to the falls.

The tracks south of the gorge are shorter and easier but, in my opinion, not as interesting. In all, Commission rangers have developed four camping tracks for a total of more than 100 kilometres as well as six day walks. If visitors intend to take a camping track they must report to the Visitor Centre and obtain a permit. It is just common sense. The experienced rangers will organise a search party for those who have not arrived at their destination by the due date.

It is possible to swim in all waterholes because only freshwater crocodiles inhabit these parts and they are not considered a danger to humans.

This is ideal country for camera work. From Crystal Falls the view across a huge chasm which begins at 17 Mile Falls and ends south of Katherine Gorge is striking. The chasm's origins have not been fully determined, but its parallel with the Martian canals is inescapable. For the chasm looks like a vast reservoir which must once have been a huge lake or wide river. All that is left is the Katherine River, puny in comparison but vital to Katherine's

The upper reaches of the Katherine Gorge.

PHOTOGRAPH BY TOM VIGUS

7000 inhabitants who get their water from this river.

The gorge and the whole area to Edith Falls is Aboriginal land. The traditional owners are the Jawoyn who, along with the Dagoman Aborigines, were the landlords until the Europeans arrived. The Dagoman have dwindled but the Jawoyn have managed to maintain a strong cultural presence in the Katherine region.

Their fight to recover their traditional lands was a burning issue in the Territory during the early 1980s. The Commission's ranger at Katherine Gorge, Alex Woods, became a Territory legend through his single-handed struggle against the land claim which he thought was prejudicial to the best interests of the majority of Territorians.

Woods lost the fight and, shortly after the claim was decided in favour of the Jawoyn, he retired to his home near the gorge. Tourists travelling there on the road from Katherine may see a sign on the left hand side proclaiming Woods's 'sacred site'. It marks the entrance to his property where he resides with his wife. An honourable man who loved the gorge and established it as one of the best run parks in the Territory.

urrounding rock faces mirrored in the tranquil waters, upstream from Edith Falls.

EDITH FALLS

*E*dith Falls is really part of the Katherine Gorge Park but deserves to be singled out for a brief mention because it is probably one of the most visited nature parks in the Katherine region or indeed in the Territory.

The reason for its popularity is simple: Edith Falls is readily accessible from the Stuart Highway 20 kilometres away by a sealed road and offers the ultimate in bush relaxation.

It is a stunning chain of falls cascading over cliffs to a deep and large pool of clear water where swimming is safe all year round.

The camping grounds offer weary travellers or families out for a camping trip a magnificent setting to spend a day or two doing nothing but swim, view magnificent sunsets and sunrises, or just read, eat and drink under generous shade.

During the Wet the falls are among the most spectacular in the Territory. There are two, the main fall which comes from a relatively low cliff and a lean but intensely bright cascade from the very top about 100 metres up.

Just before the main fall, a gurgling and happy torrent, there is a small rockhole of crystalline and cool waters nestled among rocks worn by time. It is one of the most charming and attractive water holes I have ever seen. The problem is that, to reach it, you either have to climb right up the fall itself or engage in some relatively arduous bushwalking to approach it from behind. Both involve a little risk and I would not recommend it to any but the fittest.

Edith Falls is also the goal for bushwalkers from the Katherine Gorge. It simply means that keen backpackers may start from here to the Gorge if they like. The best way to follow is up the Edith River to the marker on the wetlands where the track turns east-northeast to the 17 Mile Falls.

The same rules as for the bushwalk from the gorge apply. See the ranger, inform him/her of what you intend to do and get a permit.

I can imagine no better place for visitors fatigued from Kakadu to wash off the awesome foreboding of that park. For Edith is one of those places where you may just enjoy doing nothing more ponderous than setting up camp, walking to the pool for an absolutely delicious and refreshing swim, before a cold beer and a barbecue or, perhaps, unfolding a good novel until the sun goes down. Then it is worth another visit to the pool to see the wondrous play of the last of the sun against the red cliffs and white water.

Intriguing limestone formations, created by the weathering effects of water over thousands of years. Cutta Cutta is thought to be connected underground to Papua New Guinea.

PHOTOGRAPH BY FRANK WOERLE

86

CUTTA CUTTA CAVES

Are you curious to find out how the Great Barrier Reef may look in, say, 500 million years? Come to Cutta Cutta caves 30 kilometres south of Katherine and just one kilometre off the Stuart Highway.

This is the second largest limestone deposit in Australia (the first is in the Nullarbor Plain) and was once another great barrier reef submerged under stormy seas and teeming with marine life. The seas have long receded, the marine life perished (except for a tough little shrimp that lives a sad and blind existence in warm water at the bottom of the caves), and the live algae have given way to carbeen gums, small-leaf bauhinia and species of fig surrounded by the inevitable and ubiquitous tall tropical grasses.

But the sheer adventure of geology persists, for here you will witness the electrifying tale of colossal change that slowly shaped northern Australia. The park itself is only 260 hectares, but the limestone formation stretches 100 kilometres by 20 kilometres.

Some 500 million years ago this striking formation was indeed another barrier reef fringed by white beaches, thick jungle and tropical rainforest. Remnants of the rainforest that covered not just this area but much of the Top End can still be found here preserved by limestone firebreaks. There is an interesting small patch almost adjacent to Cutta Cutta caves.

The sea withdrew and, in time, it left behind a karst landscape associated with the so-called Tindall limestone. Erosion in limestone is unusual because it can take the form of weirdly carved towers or huge caves. The caves are the result of rain reacting with the limestone and dissolving it until large masses collapse.

Cutta itself is just one such collapse and it is startling to discover that it is the only developed cave in the Northern Territory and contains fauna rarely found elsewhere. It was named Smiths before World War 2 after a stockman who stumbled on it in 1900. During the war, when thousands of soldiers were stationed nearby and did their manoeuvres in the area, the name was changed to Sixteen Mile Cave. Its present name is the Aboriginal Jawoyn nomenclature which, in the words of a ranger, means Devil-Devil.

The Aborigines of course knew of its existence but avoided it apparently because they thought it was populated by evil spirits. They may not have been too far off the mark, for the cave contains the extremely rare ghost bat which can reach a span of almost one metre and looks like something out of a horror film.

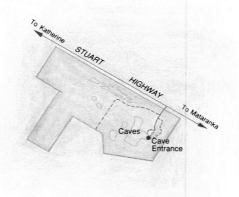

Northern blossom bats feed entirely on nectar and pollen. They hover in front of flowers, retrieving nectar with their long tongues. Found in monsoon forest and paperbark, they hang free in the trees and look like a bunch of dead flowers.

PHOTOGRAPH BY FRANK WOERLE

Ghost bats are carnivorous and exclusively cave dwellers. They eat small mammals, reptiles, birds and other bats. There is no shortage of food for them in Cutta. It is also the home of another rare bat, the golden horseshoe bat, long believed to be nearing extinction before a colony was found in Cutta Cutta.

The cave contains fairly large numbers of brown tree snakes. In fact it is only one of the very few places in the Territory, or for that matter anywhere, where visitors are guaranteed to see snakes in the wild. The common brown tree snake is a beautiful brown and white banded snake extremely proficient at climbing the smooth cave walls. The species breeds in the cave during the wet season.

So why should visitors want to come to the cave? After all, bats that look like ghosts and snakes slithering behind dark rocks may not be everybody's cup of tea. Well, for a start both are inoffensive. The bats are extremely shy of humans. And though the snakes are poisonous their fangs are positioned at the rear of their mouths and they are incapable of taking a good bite. They, and the black-headed pythons which are also found in the cave, are therefore not considered dangerous to humans.

And the cave is another world. The rangers have had the enormously good taste to avoid trick effects with the lighting system. Instead they have installed lights that, as much as possible, resemble the rays of the sun if they were able to sift through the thick crust into the cave.

They provide a spectacular show that must be seen to be appreciated. Pristine stalactites reaching down from the ceiling, gradually, ever so gradually, approaching stalagmites rising up from the floor to form columns of inimitable grace, all taking place against the backdrop of thousands upon thousands of years.

A byzantine cathedral of colours and shades, of inexplicable forms and strange shapes, greets the eye as the cave goes on and on deep into the earth. Calcite crystals and aragonites make the walls sparkle as if they had been peppered with tiny diamonds.

Then comes the end of the developed section (the real end of the cave has not yet been explored). Beyond the developed section is the entrance to yet another less civilised world, a world of utter darkness. And it is here that the blind shrimp lives.

The shrimp (previously unrecorded in Australia) is an almost extinct relic of ancient marine fauna that lives in pools deep in the cave. The only other place it has been found is in the island of Madagascar. Could this be yet another piece of evidence in favour of the theory of continental drift? The sad little animal refuses to disappear. The shrimp cannot see because it has no eyes and no pigment to colour its dark world. But it lives and that I find exciting because whatever else it may be, the blind shrimp is a tenacious fighter. It has survived since the Cambrian period. No other animal, not even that other great survivor, the crocodile, can claim a more ancient lineage.

Two new cave tours are being developed to complement Cutta Cutta itself and make the whole nature park more attractive and interesting to visitors.

They are both in the same limestone outcrop, the Guy Cave, less than two kilometres away from Cutta Cutta, an easy walk that takes visitors to the bottom of an ocean long gone. One of caves will retain the name, Guy Cave, and consists of a 100 metre walk not far from the surface. The other, Ruined Castle Cave, is exactly what the name indicates, a gloomy world deeper than Guy made up of fantastic ramparts and fortified embankments of stalagmites.

The Conservation Commission is also in the process of developing a surface walk with interpretative signs around the Guy Cave outcrop that will be linked to the two underground tours. The walk includes an area of rainforest remnant which has survived almost intact the passing of millions of years. It is a living example of what the whole of northern Gondwanaland looked like many, many years before human beings appeared on Earth.

The crystal clear waters of the Mataranka Thermal Pool are a welcome sight to the weary traveller.

PHOTOGRAPH BY FRANK WOERLE

MATARANKA

(ELSEY PARK)

The Mataranka Hot Springs near Katherine are surprising. The surrounding countryside is just what one would expect in this part of the Territory. Dusty savannah interspersed by a few trees clamouring for water. Suddenly, quite suddenly, there is an oasis of tall and luxuriant palms and pools of water so limpid you can read a book through them.

The thermal pools are much cooler than the Douglas Hot Springs and thousands of people visit them every year. In 1987, for example, about 125 000 came to experience the glory of the Mataranka Thermal Pool Nature Park, a park fully owned and managed by the Conservation Commission.

Adjacent to the park is a privately owned business venture, the Mataranka Homestead, which provides some facilities such as camping, caravan sites and limited motel accommodation. The same firm also offers restaurant facilities and runs a bar and souvenir shop.

There is no doubt in my mind that the number of visitors to this lovely nature park will increase considerably in the near future, putting even more strain not just on the park itself but on the facilities.

For a start the Mataranka thermal pools are located in a most strategic situation. It is only five kilometres from the Stuart Highway and 122 kilometres from Katherine on a sealed road. Travellers coming up the Stuart Highway from Tennant Creek have already put 667 kilometres of road behind them. They feel tired and they would like to pull off the road for a night and have a good rest before proceeding to the excitement of the Katherine Gorge or Cutta Cutta caves. What better than the Mataranka Homestead where as well as camping they can relax in a hot bath with thousands of beautiful palms around?

That is one reason why the Mataranka pools will continue to be a popular stopover for more and more people. The other reason is the recent establishment of a new park adjacent to Mataranka, the Elsey Park.

The Elsey is a delightful sequence of waterfalls, stretches of navigable river and limestone dams. The water is crystalline, its pale lime-green colour sparkling in millions of tiny bright flashes as it flows almost noiselessly through heavy forested and sandy shores.

In my view, Elsey is just about the best place for a relaxing holiday in the bush. Its camping grounds near the Roper River are superb and so are the ablution and toilet facilities. Charges are very modest and include canoe hire which allow you to explore the magnificent waterway.

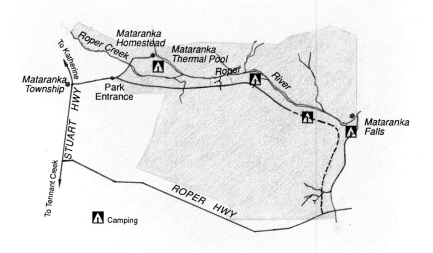

The rainbow bee-eater feeds on a wide variety of insect life. The bird batters bees and wasps against a branch to squeeze the sting out before eating them.

A preying mantis displays its perfect camouflage.

PHOTOGRAPHS BY FRANK WOERLE

The area has several sites of significance for the local Yangman/Mangari Aboriginal people. Indeed, all mature paperbark trees, which abound in the area, are sacred to Aborigines.

As well, there are extremely sensitive flora and fauna that need to be protected so that future generations can enjoy the exquisite beauty of this park as much as present-day visitors.

The limestone dams, tufas (along with the Douglas River the only ones in the Territory), are very fragile. Since much of the swimming will occur in the dams a great deal of care must be taken to protect the delicate and remarkably beautiful natural barriers.

There are plenty of freshwater crocodiles but they pose no real danger. A thorough survey has shown there are no saltwater crocodiles.

Hauser Road, named after a long-serving Territory ranger, leads off the access road to the thermal pool at Mataranka, through the park to the existing Roper Highway. It is located approximately 1500 metres from the banks of the Upper Roper, far enough to ensure that campers are not disturbed by the traffic and that the ecology of the area remains protected.

This new park has the potential to become one of the most popular destinations in the Territory. It is close to Katherine and to the Stuart Highway. It offers recreational pursuits like canoeing and safe swimming in cool and clear waters.

It is superbly scenic. It includes magnificent flora and fauna and it has significant cultural value not just for its Aboriginal content but for Europeans as well.

For example, the Territory's first Administrator, Dr J. A. Gilruth (1911–19), built a sheep dip, still in good condition, just south of the main access road.

And the Upper Roper was traversed by several European explorers. Leichhardt, on his journey from Moreton Bay to Port Essington, in fact named it and John McDouall Stuart later named the Waterhouse as well as Katherine. The park,

PHOTOGRAPH BY TOM VIGUS

The Roper River provides a permanent water source to surrounding landholders and is widely enjoyed as a popular fishing and camping area.

like Mataranka itself, is part of the historic pioneering Elsey Station.

Elsey has not yet been discovered but it will shortly although, given the size of the Park and the relative isolation of various camping sites, it is unlikely it will ever be over crowded.

Certainly for visitors driving from Tennant Creek, Elsey comes as a delightful and unexpected surprise. The last scenic place they have seen is Devils Marbles, more than 700 kilometres to the south. They have then driven across the never-never land, a vast and seemingly monotonous track broken only by a few weathered hillocks and sparse vegetation fighting for survival in an arid landscape.

And just when they think this will never end and have been condemned to an eternity of harshness, there it is, Elsey Park, an oasis in the middle of nowhere offering a chance to rest and relax. Time means nothing here. The river and the forest do, and they have an irresistible attraction that captivates the soul and weary body.

This is a gleaming, sparkling gem of a place put here by some whim of the gods.

And that is what makes the Northern Territory such a fascinating destination. Its terrible unpredictability, the whip followed by a kiss, is its nature and character. Nothing will change that.

Lush sun dappled greenery backed by splashing waters at the Daly River Nature Park.

PHOTOGRAPH BY STEVE LOVEGROVE

DALY RIVER NATURE PARK

The Daly River Nature Park is situated at the lowest crossing of the Daly River and is accessible from Darwin at all times of the year by conventional vehicles.

Fishing is undoubtedly the park's main attraction. The Daly provides an ideal habitat for the breeding of the highly prized barramundi and many other species of fish. As well as the sinister saltwater crocodiles, the river's tidal nature also brings some unsavoury characters like stingrays and the occasional shark, but that only adds to the thrill and adventure of the Daly.

There are some large and well appointed camping grounds near the crossing itself, at Robbie's Sandbar, a popular spot, and, a little further, at Brown's Creek. Downstream from there is Charlie's Creek, long favoured by Territory fishermen.

But if you happen to prefer walking and sightseeing to throwing a line over the side of a boat, you might want to take a drive to Mango Farm, a short distance from the Daly River Crossing. It is perched high on the shores and it has the most amazing collection of extremely old and luxuriantly tall mango trees (hence the name). There are also two cottages tastefully built with local stone and timber, where you can spend a relaxing night or two. As well there is a bistro (made of the same materials as the cottages) offering solid and well cooked meals for very reasonable prices. And you can take a cruise down the river in comfort. This was the high point of my visit to the Daly River Nature Park. The attempt to diversify the cattle station's operations to cater for tourism is both worthwhile and, I thought, a touching symbol of faith in the future.

Otherwise a visit to the Daly River Catholic Mission is recommended. The mission boasts a picturesque white-walled church that dominates an Aboriginal village of clean gardens and pretty houses. It is in stark contrast with other less fortunate Aboriginal settlements.

Or, if you feel a little thirsty after your efforts, you may adjourn to the Daly River pub where, over a frosty cold beer, you are likely to meet some fascinating Territory characters. The pub has a wire enclosure where a large saltwater crocodile amuses visitors by showing a magnificent set of teeth before submerging its black-brown body into slimy green water with a contemptuous lash of a well developed and muscular tail.

By all means, if you happen to be a fisherman or a photographer, go to the Daly. But if you are really looking for outstanding

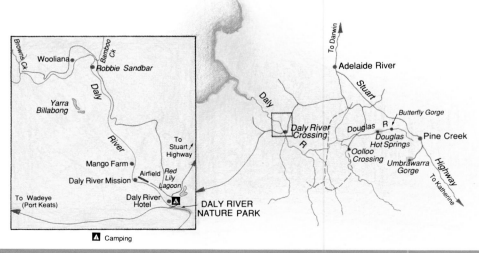

scenic surroundings and a swim look for two other places nearby, Douglas Hot Springs and the Butterfly Gorge.

Both are terrific spots. The Douglas Hot Springs, as its name indicates, consists of bubbly thermal waters that spill over into nearby lagoons and brooks. The water sings here and the camping grounds, amidst tall trees and shrubs, are very well maintained by the rangers. It is a veritable oasis among the surrounding woodland, attracting a wide variety of birds, flying foxes and other nocturnal animals.

A word of warning: the springs are hot, very hot. They are the result of volcanic activity under the ground although the water is plain rain water. The nearby escarpment acts as a catchment area for the rain which seeps to a depth of about 600 metres where it is heated before being forced back up to the surface via a fault line.

In past years thermal waters were considered to have curative powers and many people, particularly in Europe, took their holidays in one of the numerous hot springs in the old continent to revitalise their jaded bodies.

It may well be that the old theories are correct and a dip into hot mineral water is just what you need. But try it first with your big toe. I did and immediately decided against a hot bath just then. You must test the water temperature before taking a dip.

Instead the ranger took me for a short walk to a place of rare beauty where I was able to swim in lusciously cool waters. There are probably a few freshwater crocodiles around but they are too shy to mix it with humans.

The flora and fauna are of such variety that they alone deserve a patient visit. Very close to the Hot Springs there is a vast colony of bats (more like vampires judging by their size) who screeched in protest at having their daylight beauty sleep interrupted. They made their rather vulgar protest by a low-flying bombing run.

After a meticulous wash (please, no soap or detergents of any kind as they pollute the water and are harmful to fauna) we drove to the Butterfly Gorge, a short distance away through heavily wooded savannah country where quite a large number of buffaloes still

roam. Conventional vehicles can make it without much trouble in dry conditions, but four-wheel drive access is recommended.

There are two aspects to the Butterfly Gorge. The first is the fairly long walk from the parking area to the gorge itself. This was the highlight of my visit because the walk takes place through tangled and dark rainforest on the side of the murky creek below.

Although the sun shone brightly outside, there were only shadows inside dappled occasionally by a few misguided patches of intruding sunrays. A freshwater crocodile, dozing on one of the banks, was rudely awakened by our approach and splashed clumsily into the black water where it probably hugged the bottom until we had gone.

The ground was soft and mulchy with the decaying remnants of old foliage. I marvelled at the size of some of the paperbark trees, kings in a kingdom that includes lesser subjects like men weaving their way between mountainous trunks.

I thought the walk was too brief although it lasted for about half an hour. I would have liked to have spent at least a day, lost among the trees, just watching the formidable bird life and letting my mind refresh itself in contact with nature at its best.

The Butterfly Gorge itself, however, was no disappointment after the forest. It is an exquisite little gorge which derives its name from swarms of butterflies that sometimes gather there. It should be observed after a slight but difficult climb to a knoll among large and loose boulders.

You must wear sturdy footwear for the climb and certainly for bushwalking afterwards. There is an exciting walk across some very rough country which offers beautiful scenery up the secondary gorges that make up the whole system. It is well worth taking but normal precautions apply—hat, shirt, good walking shoes and water.

Swimming in the gorge afterwards is safe although I would not recommend a dip in the waters beyond the gorge itself. The creek, probably because it had not rained for a long time, appeared stagnant and

Saltwater crocodiles nest in vegetation scraped together into mounds. Eggs hatch after approximately 85 days depending on temperatures. Freshies nest in the sand along river or waterhole banks. Their eggs hatch at between 65 and 95 days.

PHOTOGRAPH BY FRANK WOERLE

covered with algae. It certainly needed a good flushing from a heavy monsoon.

On the way back you might want to take a scenic drive down the old Stuart Highway. Some great examples of Top End flora and fauna can be observed between the Adelaide River and the Daly River turnoff.

Finally, after you make it to the Stuart Highway, it is worth adjourning for a refreshing drink to Hayes Creek before moving on for a day at the old mining town of Pine Creek.

Pine Creek was the site of a gold rush more than 100 years ago. It was, in a real sense, a mini-Bendigo and Ballarat where Orientals and Occidentals met in search of the elusive stuff. At the time there were more Chinese than Europeans in the Top End and their relics remain. The town is experiencing another gold rush and its character is changing from the influx of people and new money.

The Pine Creek pub has great character. It is a pub where frontier types can be observed much like saltwater crocodiles at the Daly. They are fine at a distance but it is not advisable to tangle with them.

They make a visit to Pine Creek a must after slogging it through Butterfly Gorge or being boiled alive in Douglas Hot Springs.

Nor is this the end of an exciting adventure. Some 22 kilometres from Pine Creek over a gravel road suited for conventional vehicles there is an exceptional gorge, the Umbrawarra. It is exceptional not necessarily because it is big or striking or more beautiful or majestic than other gorges. Umbrawarra is exceptional because it offers a series of captivating sites within easy walking distance where you can swim or do nothing at all except contemplate bewitching scenery.

There is history here as well for Umbrawarra was an old tin mining region early this century and some pretty rough characters congregated there. From them emerged the first trade union in the Northern Territory, the Umbrawarra Tin Miners Association. The Territory's embryonic Labor movement and indeed the NT Labor Party itself came from those humble beginnings.

And on the way back to Darwin for a spell of civilisation, you could visit the Adelaide River war cemetery, set in manicured grounds surrounded by a profusion of crotons and other tropical shrubs and trees. Once a year, on Remembrance Day, old Territory soldiers gather here as a mark of respect for their fallen mates. It is a stately and commanding place.

A visit to the Daly region therefore includes a wide variety of experiences from fishing to photography, scenic walks, swims in gorges and therapeutic hot baths.

It is possible to do the return trip from Darwin to the Butterfly Gorge and Douglas Hot Springs in one day. How could you miss it?

Spectacular sandstone formations of Keep River National Park.

PHOTOGRAPH BY FRANK WOERLE

KEEP RIVER NATIONAL PARK

And now we come to a gem of such extraordinary quality that I was tempted not to tell anyone about it.

The Keep River National Park, about 200 kilometres west of Timber Creek and flush against Western Australia, gave me impressions that will remain deeply imprinted in my mind.

Let me tell you about those impressions first. The ranger in charge, John McCartney, affectionately known as 'Macka' throughout the service, took me to a place that had not yet been opened up for tourists although it will be by the time you read this.

It was a fair way from the station, deep into the park, in a world of tall escarpments and remarkable sandstone domes similar to those found in Western Australia's Bungle Bungles. The valley was lush with vegetation, huge boabs everywhere, and a prolific variety of trees and shrubs. Immediately ahead was a rocky promontory, the beginning of an unforgettable walk. The Jarrnarm walk, a name given to this area by the Mirriwung people who occupy the region, is well marked by star pickets topped with white markers. They took me to a world I did not even suspect could exist.

Suddenly I was at the base of a huge escarpment where graceful *Livistona* palms grew in profusion. Although the day was very hot, it was cool here. The inlet, for that is the best way to describe it, had sandy soil and was shaded by trees and vast rocky outcrops weathered into wonderful shapes by rain and wind. Woolly butt eucalypts, emu-apples, turkey bush and gardenia were all present. Green plums, billy goat plums (incredibly rich in Vitamin C), banksias, screw palms, acacias and melaleucas added to the splendid profusion of flora.

Apart from some startled birds that protested at my intrusion, there was silence. I felt as if here time had not moved since Adam and Eve walked the Garden of Eden. It belonged more in the realm of fantasy than in the real world. It was very much a journey into the kind of earth we were meant to inherit, not the one we live in.

Later I walked on to a rockhole, clearly gouged by erosive forces of water spouting fiercely over the fall during the Wet. There are fish in the rockhole: the sooty grunter,

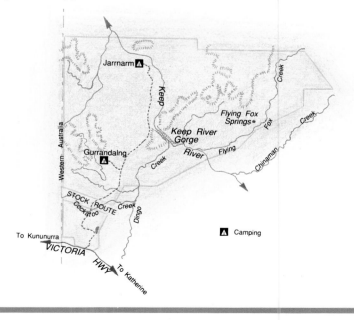

PHOTOGRAPH BY FRANK WOERLE

The screeching cries of flocks of red collared lorikeets can be heard for miles at the rising and setting of the sun.

red-tailed rainbow fish, archerfish and eel-tailed catfish.

Blue water lilies that flower during the late Wet and early Dry, paperbark trees with a few humming wasps, and luxuriant ferns growing on the surrounding walls even though this was October and there had been no rain here for several months.

A sandstone shrike-thrush called its melodious tune while I debated whether to take a swim in the wonderful pool. But it seemed such sacrilege to jump into this undisturbed mirror. I did not, and, as Macka informed me later, swimming in that specific rockhole will not be allowed because it is ecologically too sensitive.

The walk takes only an hour or so, more if you want to take your time savouring something exquisite, and it is one of the most enchanting walks I have ever taken.

Later we went for two other walks. One, very short, to a remarkable Aboriginal art gallery the likes of which do not exist outside Obiri and Deaf Adder Gorge at

Kakadu. It consists of a wide tunnel dug through the rock wall, according to Aboriginal legend, by an angry cockatoo who wanted to pass through to the other side. The explanation seemed to me at least as plausible as the geological variety which has it that wind and rain managed to carve this perfect tunnel.

Obviously the open cave served as shelter to local Aborigines escaping storms. They painted an intricate web of rock paintings on the ceiling and walls that are beautifully preserved and well worth seeing.

The other walk was more difficult and longer but a great experience as well. It is the Gurrandalng (Brolga) Walk that leads a fair way up the cliff wall and provides an unequalled view of the park. It overwhelms your senses, takes over your mind and throws your soul into confusion. How is this ... this unimaginable chaos of sandstone and conglomerate escarpments, towering cliff walls, domes, turrets, ridges, crevices, terraces, ravines and woodland

Aboriginal rock painting figures at the Cockatoo Dreaming artsite at Keep River. These figures are typical of those in the area occupied by the Mirriwung people.

The boab (bottle tree) is endemic to the north-west of the Territory.

possible? The landscape could fit several Kings Canyons. It dwarfs the spirit.

A Northern Territory geological team studied this interesting area in 1981. The dry scientific report says the Keep River Park contains parts of three major tectonic elements, namely the Halls Creek Mobile Zone, the Fitzmaurice Mobile Zone and the Victoria Basin which formed on the Sturt Block.

That is science for you. What it says to me, a layman, is that the park is the result of colossal and barely understood forces that moved the earth's crust millions of years ago in a titanic struggle to liberate the fire underneath.

For some time it was sunken beneath the sea and during this quieter time the sandstone and pudding stone formed. They were pushed to the surface by huge and unimaginable pressures.

And having done it, the forces withdrew

PHOTOGRAPH BY FRANK WOERLE

There are white-quilled rock pigeons, rock wallabies and sandstone shrike-thrushes. And as you go up you will inevitably walk into the Aboriginal Dreamtime. According to the custodians, the Mirriwung and Gadjerong people, Gurrandalng was formed by two Aboriginal men who travelled from the sea far away. They collected grass and bushes, made a large nest and commenced to jump around and make noises like the brolga. As the country listened they in fact changed into brolgas, hence the name of the place.

A senior Aboriginal man, Ginger Packsaddle, has a vast store of knowledge about the area and his own people's history that I hope I shall be able to record soon. Ginger is a grand old man whose talk at night over a sizzling steak and a couple of beers had me enthralled.

The park is, in my view, the best managed in the Territory. It is being opened up stage by stage to ensure that its unique values are not spoiled. Make sure you pick up explanatory pamphlets before you embark on an adventure that will leave a deep imprint in your mind.

A couple of concluding remarks. The Keep River National Park is adjacent to Western Australia and the spectacular Lake Argyle. A visit there is also a must.

The man-made lake is part of the Ord River irrigation scheme but is in fact one of the most spectacular expanses of water in the world. Its potential for tourism is unlimited. And from here to the famed Bungle Bungles is only about 200 kilometres.

What this means is that this area is poised for a quantum jump in visitation. The Gregory Park, a unique outback experience, picturesque Timber Creek, great fishing and sightseeing at the Victoria River, history, art, followed by the Keep River Park's awesome experience.

From there into north Western Australia to Lake Argyle and the Bungle Bungles. The whole experience is just a series of inimitable adventures.

leaving a piece of earth that is more like God's whim than the natural result of geological history.

Later, much later, sanity returned and brought vegetation and animal life to the devastated but majestic land. White-trunked eucalypts, native gardenias, ironwoods, spinifex, pindan wattles and silver-leafed grevilleas. And they are only a minute sample.

Boab trees come in many sizes and shapes. Often hollow sections of the tree fill with rain water which lasts through the dry season. The pulpy wood also holds moisture and can be beaten and squeezed to produce water.

PHOTOGRAPH BY FRANK WOERLE

GREGORY PARK

Gregory Park, about 300 kilometres west of Katherine, will be one of the largest in the Northern Territory when fully established. It will comprise more than 10 000 square kilometres of mixed country near Timber Creek, close to the border of Western Australia.

It covers all of Bullita and portions of Innesvale, Fitzroy, Auvergne, Delamere, Humbert River and Victoria River Downs stations, and it includes the Gregory's Tree Historical Reserve, a total area of just over a million hectares.

And there is a lot in it. This region marks a transition between tropical and semi-arid zones so that the geography of the place is quite distinctive. There are spectacular gorges and ranges which include significant traces of Aboriginal culture, European exploration and pastoral history. Finally there are rivers with plenty of freshwater crocodiles and abundant fishing as well as waterholes for swimming.

Access is easy. Just turn to the Bullita Station from the Victoria Highway about 12 kilometres east of Timber Creek for the start of your adventure. Four-wheel drive vehicles are needed at this stage although I understand the road is soon to be upgraded to allow conventional vehicles.

Bullita offers visitors a unique outback experience. I sat under the old homestead's verandah, a timber and corrugated iron building badly in need of renovation, and I thought I could be very happy here. Unlimited water from the river, not 20 metres away down a slight slope, good soil, plenty of shady trees, including a huge boab with DURACK, the pioneering family's name carved on it, abundant fishing, canoeing, horse riding, or just reading or doing nothing at all.

The place is made to shed the late 20th century and enter another period, more peaceful, more relaxed and more satisfying.

The river carries a good body of water and, according to the ranger, there is plenty of fish in it. There were a couple of canoes in a shed, so I assumed it was suitable for canoeing although a word of warning must be passed on. Freshwater crocodiles abound here.

Normally they are of no major concern to humans, but those at Bullita are used to being fed by hand. Just strike a couple of sticks together as you approach the river bank and you will see their thin snouts break through the placid water towards the shore. I threw a piece of bacon to one, a particularly cheeky young fellow who tried

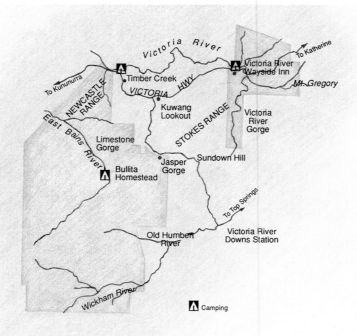

*F*reshwater crocodiles feed mainly on fish and small mammals and are not considered dangerous to humans.

PHOTOGRAPH BY FRANK WOERLE

to snap it on flight but failed. A giant yabbie grabbed it instead and rapidly hid it under a few rotting twigs for a banquet later. The croc gave me a baleful, melancholy stare, obviously begging for more. It reminded me of my dog.

One day a bright operator will open the homestead for visitors. Damper, roast beef, spare ribs, locally grown vegies, home cooked stew in the evening listening to the wild cockatoos and the eerie cries of curlews as darkness takes over.

An early morning start for a ride to the fabulous Limestone Gorge, about 13 kilometres away as the crow flies, and maybe a couple of days to explore these incredible formations and some magnificent rock art.

Then camp near the Limestone Creek where you can swim in cool waters. Make sure you announce your entry by splashing and making plenty of noise to scare away the freshwater crocs. By the way, I wouldn't try the same trick near the homestead. The crocs there are altogether too bold.

I thought the whole thing was magic. The countryside is splendid, ideal for horse riding (there are plenty of wild horses in the old station just waiting to be domesticated) and superbly scenic. You can lose yourself there, alone with your thoughts and nature.

Light a campfire at night, cook yourself a simple meal and enjoy a hot cup of coffee with maybe a little dash of rum as the shadows bring about a serene tranquility that belongs in another age.

The area has both Aboriginal and European historical significance. Traditional custodians for the area come from the Ngaliwurru, Ngaringam, Nungali, Wardaman, Jaminjung and Kurrangpurra language groups. There are many sites of significance in the area including substantial rock art sites.

Indeed the diversity and richness of art sites here rivals any other known area in the Territory or elsewhere. Those include widespread rock engravings relatively uncommon in other parts of the Northern Territory; a type of hawk trap not known to exist elsewhere; rock shelters and occupational sites of great archaeological significance; and sacred sites, five of which have already been registered.

The Conservation Commission, in consultation with the Aborigines, is in the process of recording art sites.

The European history of the area began with the discovery of the Victoria River by Captain J. C. Wickham and Lieutenant John Lort Stokes in 1839. The 1855/56 North Australia expedition led by Augustus Gregory had its base camp at Gregory's Tree Historic Reserve and Alexander Forrest's expedition traversed the Wickham River area in 1879. These explorations led to the establishment of a pastoral industry in the Victoria River District.

Gregory's Tree, a magnificent boab lording it over the Victoria River, where the explorer engraved his name and dates, has been fenced with a high wire fence to stop vandals from despoiling this valuable historical site. It is registered with the National Estate.

There is surprisingly little data on flora and fauna in this park. The rare and endangered purple-crowned wren has been identified and, of course, eucalypt and *Livistona* palms abound. But much more work has to be done before anything like a reasonably complete list of species is compiled. This is virgin country for naturalists. (University students please note: you can combine a great holiday with your studies.) The Stokes Range is a particularly important botanic region.

Apart from its obvious cultural values, however, the park is primarily a place to see, feel and do. There are two major river gorges, the Victoria River Gorge system, which is over 40 kilometres long, the river passing through the striking sandstone cliffs of the Stokes Range, towering 200 metres above, and the Wickham River Gorge in the remote southern sector of the park.

Other gorges can be found at Jasper (already mentioned), Broadarrow and Depot creeks and East Baines River.

There are also numerous freshwater creeks and waterholes, many of which are associated with narrow picturesque valleys

including Matt Wilson, Barrabarrac, Ryan, Gregory and Sullivan Creek, the tributaries to the north of Jasper Gorge and the Wickham River system. Countless and spectacular waterfalls abound immediately following heavy rain.

Other attractions include highly weathered sandstone escarpments such as Stokes Range in the northeast section of the park; numerous flat-topped ranges and landforms; and limestone features such as tower karsts and terraced hills which occur over large areas of the interior.

The Conservation Commission explains that the spectacular scenic qualities of the area together with its large size and limited accessibility, give the park a sense of ruggedness and remoteness. All too true.

It is important to note that the park is serviced by a sealed road from Katherine, National Route 1, and that the picturesque township of Timber Creek is bounded by the park. The Timber Creek annual races are a Top End event attracting visitors from all over the Northern Territory and from north Western Australia. There are two pubs in the town with caravan facilities.

Or you can camp just a short distance away on the shores of the Victoria River at Big Horse Creek, a splendid site with plenty of shade, toilets, water and barbecue facilities.

This is a park likely to prove popular on its own merits. But the added attraction is that it is also a link in the great chain of natural attractions for people wanting to explore the whole of the Top End. It is close to the Western Australian border and the road between Timber Creek and Broome is in the process of being upgraded. As places like Broome are discovered, so will the Gregory Park.

It should also be noted that the Victoria River Wayside Inn, a very good inn offering excellent service and facilities at reasonable prices and a starting point for fascinating river cruises, has been fully booked for a couple of years.

I was taken by the Gregory Park. It has a savage remoteness and a rare beauty that I found most appealing.

*L*ivistona
palms cling
to the sheer walls
along the
Victoria River.

PHOTOGRAPH BY FRANK WOERLE

Spectacular towers of the Hidden City, remarkable features of the Gulf Country.

PHOTOGRAPH BY DEREK ROFF

THE GULF COUNTRY

(FROM BORROLOOLA TO ROPER BAR)

Visitors who have seen it claim it is the eighth wonder of the world. They could be correct.

The Hidden City at the Nathan Station, about 185 kilometres north of Borroloola in the Gulf Region, is an astonishing geological formation that stretches for some 15 kilometres. The formation is much more than a city, it is a vast megapolis of razor-sharp columns, sphinx-like statues and arches put together by a marvellous natural miracle.

Here the most powerful imagination fails to conjure up words to adequately describe the unfolding scenery. Huge and graceful pillars effortlessly holding vast round ochre rocks, almost perfect cylindrical shapes jutting up high into the sky, arched gateways big enough to allow a car through, uncannily shaped human heads on the end of an upright snake. Winged monsters carved into stone forever to remind man of his fragility.

The wonder of Nathan's Hidden City is such that it has to be seen to be believed. But once there, beware, for it is said that a strange spirit lives in the maze of canyons and corridors. The spirit haunts the place and protects it. And it can be felt although never seen.

One thing is for certain. After the Hidden City all else will seem petty. This is where the senses peak, the eyes, the mind, the words. They reach a plateau of feelings and ease off afterwards because nothing can then be the same. To be sure, beauty remains in the most recondite Territory corners, but the combination of sheer and terrifying power, awesome attraction and brutal grandeur that is the Hidden City, will not be found elsewhere.

And it is difficult to reach. The Nathan River Station is in the middle of a large region between the Roper and Carpentaria highways. It can be reached by four-wheel drive vehicle during the Dry. During the Wet the station is inaccessible by road although it can be reached by air because it boasts an all-weather airstrip.

This is not a Northern Territory Park although it most surely deserves to be. The Hidden City is on private property and permission from the owners, Patrick and Roma O'Connor, is needed before visitors are allowed to the geological wonder.

The station is in the process of being developed as a tourist resort. Not only does it include one of the most striking rock formations on earth, but it is watered by the Limmen Bight River, a superb expanse of

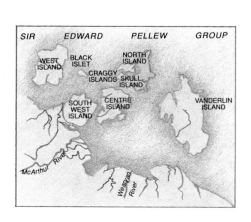

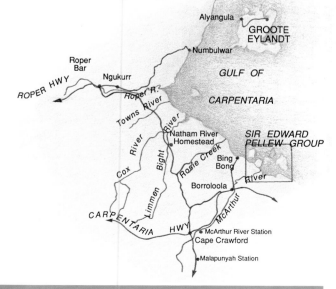

111

water where fishing is plentiful and the scenery studded with magnificent forest and rocky outcrops.

Indeed this is not the end of Nathan's potential. Not far from the homestead there is a thermal pool with crystalline waters against the backdrop of an imposing escarpment and a jungle of pandanus. And the drinking water from the station itself is arguably the finest water I have ever tasted. There is a theory that it originates in the Star Mountains of Papua New Guinea and sifts under the Gulf of Carpentaria through an immense limestone cavern. I have not been able to confirm this but there is no denying its quality. City denizens long accustomed to the dubious virtues of water piped from dams are in for a treat.

Visitors coming from the Carpentaria Highway will probably want to experience the delights of the McArthur River Station waterfalls and lagoons first. Again this is private property and permission from the owners, Mt Isa Mines, is needed. The bushwalk up the successive waterfalls is delightful and the station itself is wonderfully established with plenty of bougainvilleas and poincianas to break the aridity of the surrounding landscape.

The McArthur River Station is only 18 kilometres from Cape Crawford, the crossroads between the Carpentaria and the Tablelands highways. Some 60 kilometres before reaching Cape Crawford is the Malapunyah Station, home of one of the Territory's leading pioneering families, the D'Arcys. The original homestead is unfortunately in ruins but well worth visiting. And behind the ruins is a marvellous tropical garden with a staggering variety of plants and vegetation.

Borroloola, on the shores of the McArthur River, is rapidly being discovered by tourists as a fishermen's Mecca. Facilities to cater for the growing number of visitors are being developed including motel and caravan accommodation.

Fishing expeditions on the river itself and the Sir Edward Pellew Group of islands just off the coast can be organised.

But, at least in my view, the best part of this discovery journey is the road from Borroloola to the Roper River taking in Nathan. It is a scenic drive into true never-never land culminating in experiences that can never be forgotten.

Finally you will reach the Roper River, another favourite with fishermen. This is an interesting place, and not just because of the abundant fish.

First, history. Here Aborigines fought fiercely to ward off the foreign invasion. Hell's Gate was the site of several bloody ambushes of European and Chinese gold prospectors. Graves dot the landscape and they tell the story of that extraordinary struggle which concluded, despite the remarkable valour of the Aborigines, in victory for the newcomers. A melancholy headstone at the old police station site reads: 'C. H. Johnson Speared by blacks June 1875.' No one knows what the retaliation for the killing was. And there were many, indeed very many, such incidents.

Perhaps the Aborigines took their dead to a sacred burial site nearby, a strikingly beautiful rocky outcrop guarding the entrance to a large cave. Three large monoliths, uncannily shaped like human heads, are placed strategically, almost as if by design, in front of the cave's mouth. There are still plenty of human bones inside, the shins split and painted in various colours. This is also a major rock art site, unfortunately unrecorded as yet and certainly unvisited.

I am not aware that any Government instrumentality or Aboriginal organisation has taken guardianship of this site. It must be protected for its obvious cultural and historical value.

A police station (now on the national register) was established in Borroloola in 1886 to control its rowdy nature and, sure enough, some of the worst excesses quietened down but the Gulf is still the Gulf, its quintessential frontier character unchanged.

Escarpments, strange and unexplainable rock formations, clear rivers, gnarled and angry forests. What a backdrop for the larger than life Aborigines and settlers that fought to the death for this land!

The region is definitely a must.

No account of the Gulf Region would be complete without mention of one of the Conservation Commission's most recent additions to the Territory national estate.

It is North Island, in the Sir Edward Pellew Group of islands, a 5421 hectares pearl eighty kilometres north-east of Borroloola and thirty-five kilometres north-east of McArthur River mouth. The Park will soon be named Barranyi National Park which is held in freehold title by the Barranyi Aboriginal Corporation and leased to the Commission for ninety-nine years.

There is a small unused airstrip on North Island which I have no doubt will be upgraded at some stage to bring visitors quickly and in comfort. Personally, I prefer the longer but infinitely more pleasurable boat journey from Borroloola down the McArthur River to its wide mouth.

Just outside the mouth there are two rocky promontories, like sentinels guarding all approaches to the river. They are Black Craggy and White Craggy, on whom the setting sun plays tricks making them change colour from deep purple shadows to creamy white, hence their names.

It was getting late so we decided to camp for the night on Black Craggy before continuing our trip to North Island. Old Man Johnston, a Barranyi Aboriginal from Borroloola, owns this little island and he told me stories on the beach while the huge moon slowly rose over the sea and the fire became embers. The stories took us both to a past populated by human beings, plants and animals that understood each other and lived in harmony.

The harmony almost certainly had to do with a relatively abundant past for here fish and game abound. The choppy seas were alive with mackerel next day, literally boiling with millions of fish on whom sea eagles, gulls and other predators swooped with glee. It was an astounding spectacle in the midst of splendour as the boat threaded its way through the chain of islands to the north.

Very soon our little party, which included the Conservation Minister, Mike Reed, approached Paradise Bay on North

North Island, an unspoilt paradise in the Gulf of Carpentaria.

Island itself. It is aptly named, a half moon shaped beach of fine sand stretching for about two kilometres from a remarkably beautiful outcrop of limestone rocks in the north to a series of small hillocks in the south. It nestles happily shaded in part by thickets of casuarinas and vines.

The vines are a rare and vulnerable plant community in the Gulf and they are probably crucial for the survival of some animal species which occur on the islands. So far there have been records of 193 bird species (eight of them never recorded on the mainland), as well as forty-two species of reptile including five turtle species on the endangered list.

Also, four of the twenty-six mammal species recorded for the Pellew Islands have not been seen on the mainland in recent times, underlining the importance of conservation here.

These islands are therefore important biological laboratories, in that plant and animal species can be studied almost in isolation and without the complicating intrusion of many factors on the mainland. The Island should be mainly a conservation marine park where visitation is restricted to about today's level or, with a few qualifications, a slight increase.

All along East Arnhem Land, there are islands and coastal areas with much sturdier environments where tourist development catering for very large numbers is possible. It is not possible on North Island. This little fragile Island would wither and die with excessive visitation.

The spectacular Devils Marbles are one of nature's wonders. Truly magnificent tors sit atop large boulders.

PHOTOGRAPH BY DEREK ROFF

114

BARKLY TABLELANDS

(D E V I L S   M A R B L E S)

*M*y companion, David Fuller, and I arrived at Devils Marbles at 9:30 pm under a full moon. We had not intended to reach the world famous landmark about 100 kilometres south of Tennant Creek this late. But a fair distance from Tennant, at Renner Springs, our car blew a tyre.

It took a relatively long time to have it fixed which gave me the opportunity to sit on a mound by the side of the road and absorb the surroundings.

Just in front was the thin stretch of bitumen that Territorians know as the Track, the Stuart Highway, the Territory's umbilical cord connecting it to the rest of Australia. Ahead was a vast plain stretching 360 degrees and broken only by a couple of

jagged knolls undeserving of their name. The vegetation was sparse and scraggly, hard, just as hard as the country of their birth.

It was indescribably beautiful. The soft warm breeze blew all the way from the Tanami Desert bringing with it a twang of dry gidgee wood, the wood that burns with the heat of stars. A few wispy clouds were beginning to turn soft pink out in the west where the sun had started to set. The black ants at my feet hurried home for the night.

There was not a single car on the road, not a telltale sign of civilisation or human habitation anywhere. For all I knew the world had ceased to exist, history had come to a stop. The immensity of it all, its sheer grandeur and splendid majesty

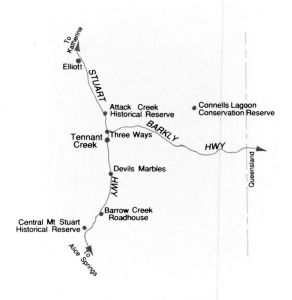

The Devils Marbles provide a relatively cool and sheltered refuge for desert fauna—including nesting fairy martins, sand goannas and zebra finches.

PHOTOGRAPH BY STEVE LOVEGROVE

116

overwhelmed me for an instant.

Shortly afterwards we were treated to one of the most indelible spectacles in my life. As the sun finally went down in the west in a magnificent blaze of colour, a full moon appeared in the east wrapped in a dark blue haze. It was of such awesome beauty that David and I stared spellbound. We did not talk for that would have broken the magic spell.

But even this unequalled show did not prepare me for what I was to experience later that evening. We arrived as the moon had conquered the sky, sending a pale ghostly light on to the vast landscape below. We immediately made camp at the foot of one of the huge Marbles. Present camping facilities are limited, but there are plans for a caravan park nearby.

Bathed by opaque moonlight I set a small table, put out my sleeping bag, and sat on a folding metal chair to gaze in wonder at the grotesque shapes all around.

For the Devils Marbles is a natural phenomenon found only in that remote corner of the Territory and nowhere else in the world. Nothing anywhere remotely resembles the Marbles, the gargantuan round blocks of red and grey granite perched on top of one another or carelessly strewn over a large area of bare ground.

The formation just ahead, not ten metres away, particularly fascinated me. It consisted of a huge rounded base with two bizarre, insanely large pebbles on top. The whole thing defied both the neat formulas of architectural design and the laws of nature. Yet they had been there for eons and will remain in place long, long after I travel to Nirvana.

Devils Marbles is for disbelievers and for monks. The first group can always try to explain the whole thing through a careful study of geology and come to their own conclusions. This has been done and the proper explanations recorded in books. They are immensely unsatisfactory in that they do not deal with what seems to me the most important question: why do these strange geological forms exist only in this very limited piece of ground? There is not even a hint of them in the surrounding countryside, not a single warning, nothing similar.

The second group would probably be confused as to whether the Marbles were put there by God or, as the locals presume, the Devil.

Scientists say they all come from a giant granite formation which crystallised about 2000 million years ago. They do not say why or how it crystallised. Once it happened, however, the huge mass was ready to break into pieces. The pieces, weathered over thousands of years by wind and rain, are in fact the Marbles.

It seems to me that Aborigines have a far more satisfactory explanation. They say the weird rocks are in fact nothing more than the fossilised eggs of the Rainbow Serpent which features in all Dreamtime stories.

But it does not matter. What matters is they are there for visitors to see and wonder about.

The Marbles have been an object of fascination for European visitors since they were first sighted. The founder of the Royal Flying Doctor Service, John Flynn, a revered Territory pioneering figure, asked to be buried under one of the Marbles. A giant boulder was carried to his grave in Alice Springs where it stands guard to the end of time.

The Devils Marbles are a geographical marvel. Pictures just do not reflect the stateliness and splendour of the outcrop, its massive size or its weird quality. Nothing but physical sightseeing can do that.

Glowing ochre in the late afternoon light, the Olgas epitomise the awesome majesty of Australia's Red Centre.

PHOTOGRAPH BY STEVE LOVEGROVE

THE RED CENTRE

*T*he desert sand of Central Australia is a rich red ochre. Above, the endless sky is a deep cobalt blue. In winter the temperature may well be below freezing, but at the height of summer the midday sun can force the mercury to an incredible 50ºC.

Australia's Red Centre has been a frustrating challenge for thousands of years. Many have perished trying to cross its trackless wastes, some in search of vital water sources, many lured by dreams of fabulous wealth and precious metals.

Humankind has now conquered the great Australian deserts with jet aircraft, sealed highways and railway tracks ... but it took 200 years! Visitors still dare not venture far from the roadway.

Today's explorer to the Red Centre will find some of the world's most magnificent scenery ... rugged gorges, gentle oases, delicate wildflowers. Truly an incredible experience!

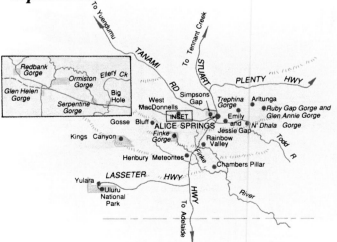

Weedy Waterhole in the Davenport and Murchisson Ranges. One of the many waterholes and waterways in the area which make this new national park such a surprisingly attractive destination.

PHOTOGRAPH BY CONSERVATION COMMISSION

DAVENPORT AND MURCHISON RANGES

If you have ever wondered what the country east of Devils Marbles looks like but have not had the opportunity to find out, now is your chance. The Davenport and Murchison Ranges, two impressive landmarks near Tennant Creek, have been added to the national estate in the Northern Territory and link the more classic Central Australian offerings, such as Ruby Gap or the Dulcie Range, with the Top End.

The country here still has far more in common with the Red Centre than with the north, but there are slight differences that deserve recognition in a new national park of stature. This is what Davenport–Murchison will become in time.

Right now, the area remains remote and isolated. Apart from an initial brief survey by three Conservation Commission Wildlife Researchers, Johnson, Latz and Fleming, with the help of two local Aborigines, Sandy Jampijimpa and Albert Japiljarri, this area is virtually unexplored and certainly unvisited.

The Davenport and Murchison Ranges lie roughly parallel to one another and run southeast for about 180 kilometres, with the more northerly point on the Stuart Highway about 40 kilometers south of Tennant Creek. The new 2000 square kilometre national park takes on parts of McLaren Creek Station (which straddles the Stuart Highway and includes Devils Marbles) and Kurundi Station.

Perhaps the Commission's survey tells the story of this area best: 'With some exceptions, most of the areas with scenic and recreational appeal are presently inaccessible to all but the most adventurous visitors.'

And that, in my view, is the park's greatest attraction. It is difficult to get to, but when you finally make it, you can be sure you won't be disturbed by anything other than the screech of cockatoos and the rustle of wind against rocky outcrops and gum trees.

You are probably going to have mixed feelings about this area. On the one hand, the approaches are not particularly appealing. You are confronted by the terrible and uncompromising nature of this country. No matter where you look, there is no respite. The intimidating vastness of the Territory unfolds before your eyes.

Powerful hills, eroded and squat, stare down at you. They have been there for millions of years, they have seen it all, the foibles of nature, the changing seasons, greenhouse effects and ice ages, great water and unending dry. And now they see you

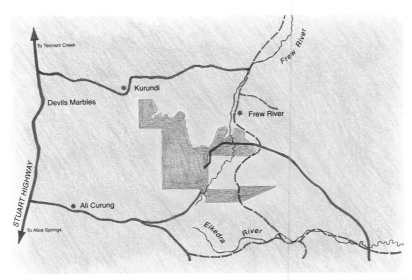

venturing into their dominion and do not like it, that is plain.

But a strange metamorphosis occurs as you drive deeper and deeper into the country. Gradually the land gives way and does so in a welcoming fashion, as if it understands you are now a partner in this huge loneliness, not an intruder to be frightened away.

Stand on a ridge and let the hot wind come to you from the ranges like an unbroken sough. That is their talk. What they are saying may not be clear for a while, but you must be patient, for the hidden message will become clear. It will tell you an amazing story if you are prepared to listen, and the story has to do mainly with the secret of beauty. For here you learn that the gap between loveliness and ugliness does not exist and has always been artificial.

If you want kind green meadows and clear streams under benign skies, do not come here. This country does not have a pretty face, nor even an attractive one. It is pock-marked, ravaged by time, and old.

But it is also immensely resilient, tough, durable, and generous. This land is ugly and radiantly beautiful at the same time, and it will let you touch it with a soft caress if you care. Only if you care.

I think that is the secret of the Davenport–Murchison Ranges. It will not surrender easily, perhaps not at all, but if it does, you will discover things that you had never suspected exist. Among them, with some luck, all those pieces of your soul carelessly discarded in the business of living, and this is not so unusual on the Territory's forbidding soil. However, you may be more interested in the history of man here than in the play of natural geological or climatic forces.

The Davenport–Murchison marks a boundary for the three major Aboriginal groups in the region. The Warramungu people occupied the northern catchment area as far as the Frew River which, in turn, marked the beginning of the Aljawarra people's country to the south-east. The southern part in the Wycliffe Creek catchment area belonged to the Gaididj people, who are related to the Warlpiri to the west and to the Arrente to the south-east.

Aboriginal mythology is alive here. One of the gorges in the ranges, Inkangarti (or Whistle-duck Gorge), is known to be associated with the Kestrel Dreaming, and in the early days of white settlement, was said to have been used as an escape route by Aborigines fleeing mounted parties of whites, who were unable to get their horses through the gorge.

Another gorge, Tijirlinyi, is also associated with the Dreamtime. Aborigines in the area say that Dreamtime people passing through Tijirlinyi gorge found that they became trapped when the cliff faces closed up behind and in front of them. Indeed, at one stage of the traverse through the gorge, the bends make it appear as if the way ahead is impassable and the way back closed off.

At present, the Conservation Commission is engaged in gathering more information about Aboriginal lore in this region. Artifacts relating to earlier occupancy remain, and Dreamtime stories concerning various aspects of the country persist among Aborigines who have kept their cultural associations. It is very important that the Commission continues to gather the pieces that make up the area's Aboriginal history.

John McDouall Stuart was the first European explorer to the region in 1860, but it was the establishment of an Overland Telegraph Station at Tennant Creek, in 1872, that encouraged exploration of the ranges.

The first official party to explore the Davenport Ranges was led by the SA Government geologist H. Browne, who reported on mineralisation of the Hatches Creek area in 1896. But already pastoral lands were being occupied. Cattle stations had been established on Frew River, Elkedra River and Murray Downs Creek in the early 1890s, but a series of bad droughts, distance from markets and 'the blacks causing endless trouble …' (Davidson A. 1905— *Explorations in Central Australia*—SA Parliamentary Paper No 27/1905) led to them being abandoned.

Alan Davidson conducted the first detailed exploration of the area in 1898 while looking for gold for the Central Australian Exploring Syndicate. His report to the South Australian Parliament is interesting, because it lists the geology and the topography of the region as well as some incidental, but useful, observations on biology.

Otherwise, the area's non-Aboriginal history is not notable or very much different from most other parts of the Territory. A man called Henty had a holding on the Frew River in 1929 but was murdered at Hatches Creek, again not an uncommon event in the Land of the Never Never. This area is best known for its tungsten, wolfram and scheelite deposits, which were first mined as early as 1913.

But the Tennant Creek region is best known for goldmining, and this has certainly influenced the Davenport–Murchison Ranges. Two small goldmines are being actively worked on Kurindi Branch Creek and Opal Creek.

Mining attracted some unruly elements that needed to be brought to heel from time to time. This meant a police presence, and what a lonely job it must have been. An example is provided by the Old Police Station built on an attractive corner of the waterhole of the same name on the Frew River (reasonably easy to access from Tennant Creek). The station is now reduced to ruins, a pile of scattered rocks that once housed a lone policeman who kept a lookout on top of a small ridge and rode incredibly long distances in one of the most desolate and largest beats in the world. They are touching ruins, because of what they tell us about the impetus and the extremities of Australian pioneering expansion.

The waterhole, about 1 kilometre long in the Dry, is probably permanent and holds a good stock of spangled perch. The gorge above is one of the most attractive in the area and has many large waterholes.

Further north, there are five rockholes with important scenic and recreational value, but only one, Japa Rockhole, is accessible by road, via a rough track from the north-east.

That is pretty well the story about the whole park, where large waterholes and scenic gorges abound, but are seldom seen because access is difficult.

The flora is not spectacular, although there are 11 land systems in this area. It consists of snappy gums in the foothills, soft spinifex on the rocky hills and river red gums and occasional dense thickets of teatrees (melaleuca) near watercourses. There are also coolibahs in the better watered areas.

A total of 435 plant species have been recorded for this large area, about the same number as are known to exist in the much smaller Simpsons Gap National Park in the Macdonnell Ranges. The only thing of note here is that they represent an overlap zone between Central Australian species and northern monsoon species.

The Conservation Commission has also recorded 18 Australian mammals and 6 introduced mammals, but the survey was not exhaustive and much more work needs to be done before we know exactly what the area contains. Some species, such as the golden bandicoot, are believed to have disappeared, perhaps as the result of Aboriginal hunting.

As well, the Commission has recorded 105 bird species generally representative of the region. Mostly, they are arid zone birds but a modest influence from the Top End was seen in waterbirds, which included species such as the glossy ibis and black-necked stork. I am glad to say that I saw plenty of green budgies there. Budgerigars have been rare or absent recently.

Some 52 species of reptiles have been recorded, including geckos, legless lizards, dragon lizards, goannas, skinks, pythons and other snakes.

Surprisingly, the area appears to be a rich habitat for fish and some seven species have been recorded, including spangled perch and freshwater shrimp. At Police Station Waterhole, enough spangled perch can be fished for a substantial breakfast.

To conclude, the Davenport–Murchison Ranges together are the best-watered region in Central Australia. Waterholes and rockholes are numerous and diverse in the 180 kilometre long Ranges. The Davenport–Murchison Ranges are not for everybody. This is very demanding Central Australian landscape. It is demanding on the spirit and on the body. But the reward is more than just a quick talking point over a picture when you get back home. In fact, you might not even want to talk about it.

Peregrine Gorge in the Dulcie Ranges is remote and wild, showing off its unique Central Australian colours which are best viewed at sunset.

PHOTOGRAPH BY ALAN GINUS

DULCIE RANGE

or those with some familiarity with Latin, 'Dulcie' may mean a number of things, all associated with sweetness and gentility. But there is nothing sweet or gentle about the Dulcie Range.

The range is the main feature of one of the Northern Territory's newest parks, comprising about 2000 square kilometres of bare and seemingly arid and angry country about 220 kilometres north-east of Alice Springs. You probably have heard about Outback Australia, have read about it and seen it in pictures and documentaries. You may think you know a lot about the history of pioneers and explorers; you identify with their struggles and their epic journeys.

The Dulcie Range provides you with a unique opportunity to experience everything that you think you know. More than that, it brings you close to a prehistoric civilisation, one whose mysteries are still to be unravelled and which may yet teach us much.

The European history of the area is barely 100 years old and is not particularly remarkable, for it is repeated in many parts of the Northern Territory. The first recorded European to this area was an explorer, Charles Winnecke, who visited the Oorabra Rockhole in 1878. Really, the only thing of interest that Winnecke recorded was the highest point in the range, Mt Ultim (about 612 metres above sea level), which he used as a landmark.

In 1896, the South Australian Government geologist, H. Y. L. Brown, investigated the Oorabra Range and then travelled to the northern face of the Dulcie Range. By then, some hardy prospectors had entered this area, although they left few or no records of their findings.

The only other official visit to the area was in 1912 by R. H. Macpherson, second in command of the 1911/12 Barclay Macpherson Expedition, which passed through the Dulcie Range along Ooratippra Creek. They recorded several waterholes and little else.

In 1916, T. E. Day, Chief Surveyor of the Northern Territory surveyed the area and it is generally believed he named the Range after his daughter, although this has not been confirmed.

Since then, the only event of any note occurred when the eminent geologist, C. T. Madigan, travelled along Ooratippra Creek through the Dulcie Range in 1937 to examine an unusual rock, later known as the Huckitta Meteorite (an important Aboriginal men's sacred site).

Parts of the Dulcie Range are now included in several pastoral stations and grazing is the main industry in the area

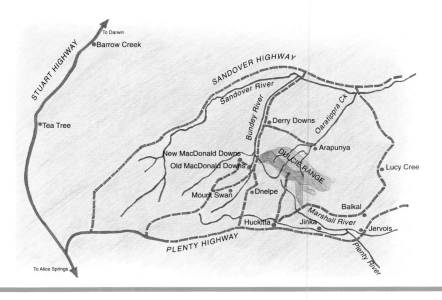

dating back to 1913, when Huckitta Station was established. This means that if you venture here, you are venturing into a virtually virgin and practically uninhabited area.

Allow me a brief comment. Recently, I watched a television documentary on the effects of tourism in various destinations around the world. There were wall-to-wall people everywhere. They thronged and palpitated. They intruded everywhere. Beaches were overcrowded, as were museums, buildings, streets and churches. Everywhere, people elbowed people for a tiny place. If you are fed up with that, you will want to come to the Dulcie Range. Here you will find few people, or perhaps no one, and it will probably remain that way in our lifetime, because access is difficult and when you get there you won't find any comforts except those you bring with you.

This is true wilderness, but it is (for me) something more than that. There was an ancient civilisation here many, many thousands of years ago (no one knows how many, because there have been practically no archaeological studies of the area).

A Conservation Commission report of the area puts it this way: 'The Dulcie Range has, for some time, been considered an area rich in Aboriginal cultural resources. However, to date only a very small part of the Range has been surveyed'.

The Range is within the tribal boundary of the Alyawarre Aboriginal people. The Eastern Arrente (sometimes referred to as Arunta) people from the south also have associations with the area. Their ancestors have left many traces of their culture and life, including innumerable stone artifacts which can be found in caves and on ledges. Do yourself (as well as heritage) a favour if you visit this area. Leave it undisturbed and do not collect ancient stone tools for your home collection.

The Conservation Commission has received many letters from people around Australia and overseas returning small pebbles and rocks that have been picked up as souvenirs and which they claim have brought them bad luck. You do not have to believe in the power of palaeolithic artifacts such as stone flakes or in the sacredness of some rocks. But you are still strongly advised to leave everything as you find it, so that archaeologists can conduct a proper study of the area.

There are no sacred sites registered in this region at present, although the entire Oorabra Gorge outcrop area has been proposed for registration. There are 86 sites of huge cultural significance recorded, featuring predominantly hand stencils, hand prints, implement stencils and designs of paintings.

One, of a head shield at the Oorabra water-hole, is probably the oldest example of rock art I have ever seen (with the possible exception of paintings found at the top of the Fitzmaurice River Gorge in the Top End). Significantly, the Oorabra Rockhole is also home to three important sites associated with Rain, Bandicoot and Snake Dreamings. Huckitta Station itself was named after a major Aboriginal Dreaming story which, paradoxically, means the End of Dreaming. This is where it stops.

Aboriginal people have been here for a long time. They go back to an era when this country looked very different and when other climatic and geographical imperatives ruled. Their paintings sometimes indicate war, but also often speak of something much more simple and wonderful—the curiosity of the human mind about the world around.

But you may not be interested in history or archaeology. All you want is to spend a few days in splendid isolation, recharge your batteries, as it were, away from the humdrum of life and in contact with the Outback.

The Mutcer Rock at the Dulcie Range appears in front of your eyes like an old Mayan temple worn by age, rain and wind.

PHOTOGRAPH BY ALAN GINUS

You have come to the right place. Here, there are sheltered gorges, major watercourses and springs, and scenic rock outcrops. If you let your imagination run wild, you can think of the colossal forces at work over millennia that have shaped and made this country.

A total of ten large gorges (over 1 kilometre long) and nine smaller gorges have been surveyed and recorded. And that is only the beginning. Aerial photographs show that a similar number, if not more, occur in the unsurveyed parts of the Range. Most gorges are scenically attractive and provide sheltered settings.

Gorge sites are, well, gorgeous. They range from coloured cliffs, sheer rock faces and scree or boulder slopes to broken, stepped rock faces and steep rock slopes. Scalloped or domed overhangs and caves are common, often showing areas of striking coloured sandstone. And you will find springs and permanent waterholes in most gorges, often in an attractive setting of lush (and some-times unrecorded) vegetation.

The larger gorges, usually the most scenic, are long narrow gorges cut into the edges of the Range and upland plateaus. They are generally 60–100 metres deep with striking entrances (such as those in the West Macdonnells) flanked by high rocky escarp-ments. Their deep narrow ridges are among the coolest and most sheltered sites in the Range. Examples include Split Rock, Picton Springs, Peregrine, North and Pound gorges.

The major watercourses are the Ooratippra and Arapunga creeks in the Range, and Oomoolmilla and Oorabra creeks to the south-east. A visit to the Ooratippra Creek is strongly recommended. It is a well-vegetated channel containing several permanent and semi-permanent waterholes even during the months of the Dry. But the thing that I find most attractive is the impressive collection of rocky

outcrops that speak of the passing of years and wind and rain.

The most notable, in my view, is the Oorabra Outcrop, an area of bare ochre rock slabs more than 5 square kilometres south-east of the Range. It appears from the distance as a series of broken rocky benches. Closer, it is entirely like one of the numerous 'hidden cities' found in the Territory, made up of stunning rock faces, steep rock slopes, cliffs, large overhangs and caves, rock pillars and arches. The whole eerie effect is compounded by crops of stunted ghost gums, where a few giant euros graze.

Ghost gums, cypress pines, acacias and figs are among the more common trees in the area, which is the habitat of 335 discovered species of which 21 are rare or relict species.

The fauna is just as interesting. There are rare fish in the waterholes, including spotted grunter, rainbow fish and sail-fin perchlets. Generally, though, the waterholes here tend to be polluted by cattle, and fishing is not a recommended activity.

Conservation Commission wildlife experts have also recorded 31 species of reptiles, but this is likely to be very conservative and more species will be discovered as the area becomes better known.

The same surveys have identified 84 bird species, with a further 20 species reported to the Biological Records Scheme. If you happen to be a birdwatcher you will delight in dusky grasswren, spinifex bird, striated parladote and peregrine falcons, which are pretty rare in these parts. The spinifex pigeon, normally in chattering groups, painted firetail, little wood-swallow and spotted bowerbirds (the bunch of thieves that they are) can be observed in rocky outcrops.

There are also 17 native mammal species

here. Some evidence has been uncovered which suggests that ghost bats and pale field rats lived here in the past, though they are unlikely to inhabit the area now. The ghost bat is thought to be extinct in Central Australia.

So there you have it. History and scenery combined with a powerful sense of being alone in the universe. The stars are brighter here and so is the morning sky and the sunsets. I hope this place will never become fashionable.

The White Range Cemetery at Arltunga, with graves dating from the gold mining days of the late nineteenth century.

PHOTOGRAPH BY DEREK ROFF

130

ARLTUNGA

*N*ow, I don't know how you feel about history but, for me, history is everything. It determines what we are, the way we think and what we are about to become.

It also defines basic concepts such as whether we are free or subjugated, visionary or narrow, and whether we have a future as a nation. For history, more than anything else, is our inheritance and most valuable heirloom.

That is why I looked forward so much to the short journey from Trephina Gorge to the old gold mining settlement at Arltunga.

The Arltunga Historical Reserve is only 110 kilometres from Alice Springs and just 50 kilometres east of Trephina but it might well be a lifetime away from both. The hustle and bustle of the lovely Central Australian capital and the quiet beauty of Trephina have nothing to do with Arltunga.

Here ghosts live. They belong to the men who defied all odds and walked or rode immense distances lured by gold. As had been the case some 30 years earlier in New South Wales and Victoria, alluvial gold was discovered in this remote corner of Central Australia in 1887. Word spread fast and the rush was on. Miners from all over Australia arrived, many pushing their barrows, others with nothing but what they could carry on their backs, and some, the lucky ones, with horses, mules or camels. At one stage the area supported about 3000 people.

They are still there. I could feel them groaning under the weight of heavy pans, sweating as they dug impossible tunnels with their blunt picks and shovels—and sometimes dynamite—brawling and fighting. And when the bitter months of winter came, bringing winds that cut and freezing nights, they built small semicircular stone windbreaks to shield them from the cold southeasterlies. They are still in the area as a mute testimony of hard times and tough men.

But above all I could sense them talk of their dreams, all about to come true with the next shovelful, and the next ... tomorrow.

The heritage, restored with great care by the Conservation Commission, is rich indeed. It includes the ruins of a number of stone buildings and rusted machinery imported from Bendigo, Victoria, and other old goldrush places. Some of the original diggings have also been cleaned up and opened for visitors who are welcome to clamber down metal ladders to the bottom and meander through the short dark corridors that contained gold.

Let us first look at the people. Those who came seeking their fortune had to travel daunting distances through harsh, sometimes impossible, terrain. From the Oodnadatta railhead, a good and familiar landmark, they had to travel 600 kilometres to the goldfields, more often than not on

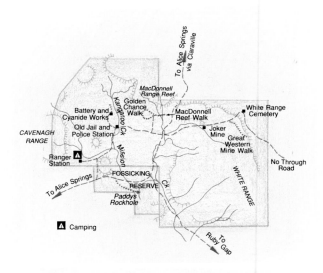

PHOTOGRAPH BY DEREK ROFF

*A*rltunga's stone-walled cell block, temporary home to many a miscreant in the early days of the township.

foot. Alice Springs, which they struck on the way, was then only a tiny outpost which expanded rapidly when it became the supply depot for Arltunga. Arltunga, by the way, officially became Central Australia's first town.

Who were these men? They were the cream of Australia, the dreamers, visionaries, the dissatisfied and the discontented. Individualists. Men of indomitable courage and great physical stamina. People who dared.

The vast majority were Australian born, but others came from overseas. Very few made their fortunes. Many stayed on and became Territorians—graziers, pastoralists whose descendants still work the land. Others remained forever, their bodies mercifully laid underground in a bleak little cemetery where nothing remains except some nameless and curiously touching headstones.

Alluvial gold mining continued in many dry creek beds for 20 years. Reef gold was discovered in the nearby White Range in 1897 resulting in higher yields. But by 1912, little activity remained in either area and the battery only operated intermittently after 1913.

Since then there have been sporadic attempts to mine the area, including a small rush during the 1930s Depression. In recent years, however, there has been an upsurge of mining activity in the White Range area.

The major historical destinations within the park are the Government Battery and Cyanide Works, the Old Police Station and Jail, Crossroads area and Cemetery, Joker

PHOTOGRAPH BY DEREK ROFF

ection of the preserved Government Stamp at Arltunga.

Mine and Great Western Mine, and the White Range Cemetery.

The government works remain but there is little evidence of the old shanty town at the Crossroads except an unidentified stone building in fairly good condition. The government battery was the administrative centre of the township and buildings there have been substantially restored.

I liked the Old Police Station most of all. The stone and corrugated iron building has a good verandah overlooking a large landscape which is both aesthetically appealing and sound.

Walking tracks take visitors through the old ore Battery and Cyanide Works, the Police Station precinct, old mine workings and residential areas. The ranger in charge is a veritable store of information and will give you a guided tour of the lot.

For the more adventurous walker, sweeping views of the surrounding ranges can be obtained by climbing any of the higher hills within the park.

By the way, if you feel like doing a little fossicking of your own, forget it. The use of metal detectors is prohibited on the reserve. However, a fossicking reserve is located just outside the park boundaries.

Pets, like almost everywhere else, are not permitted. And of course all plants and animals within the park are protected, except the donkeys, of which there seems to be a fair abundance.

Finally, why not a visit to the Arltunga pub? It has true Territory style and the beer is frosty cold. The pub, by the way, offers good camping and caravan facilities for visitors.

The ranges of Central Australia were cut in many places by the flow of ancient watercourses, leaving a long chain of shady gorges.

PHOTOGRAPH BY NEIL PHILLIPS

RUBY & GLEN ANNIE GORGES

I don't want to mince words or be vague about this. Ruby Gorge is the best gorge in Central Australia. Forget every other gorge anywhere. Ruby is the grandad of them all. It dwarfs them, makes them insignificant and, from its lofty heights, looks upon the rest of the world with something like indifference.

From Arltunga you head off towards the east-southeast on a passable road to the cattle station of Atnarpa, then a course slightly further south to Ruby, all in all about 154 kilometres northeast of Alice Springs or two hours of strictly four-wheel drive hard driving from Arltunga.

This is real, no-nonsense bush. You are heading into the wilds of Central Australia where almost anything is possible and indeed likely.

The landscape, if anything, gets more rugged and more impossibly beautiful. On rounding a worn hill, I was confronted with a mass of tumbled sierras, hazy blue, green and yellow, which forced me to stop and stare in absolute awe. This was supposed to be the desert where hardy spinifex and stunted shrubs can make a home but nothing else thrives.

A short while later the Ruby Gorge appeared. Eight kilometres of winding, meandering corridor with cliffs as high as tall buildings broken by huge ledges, caves, crevices and ravines, all adorned with trees and an inifinite variety of vegetation.

The floor is a sandy, rocky highway, a broad avenue fringed by absurdly fragile ghost gums and river red gums. Twisted, stunted specimens of ghost gums clinging to the rock face giving out soft white powder when rubbed. The powder is used by Aborigines for ceremonial body painting.

The river red gums, named because of their rich red timber, house thousands of birds. One of the trees had fallen near the gorge's entrance and three young boughs grew from the main trunk.

Further on there were bloodwoods which bleed thick red sap when struck by an unthinking axe. They bear an apple-like fruit that Aborigines eat as bush tucker.

PHOTOGRAPH BY DEREK ROFF

Whitewoods were there, too, not a tree at all but shrubs ten metres high whose pale timber is favoured by Aborigines to carve into snakes and goannas.

Fuchsia bushes with their umbrella canopies, dark wattles, witchetty bushes, silver cassias and native figs. They are all there at Ruby Gorge. In many banks delicate grasses give the impression of having been freshly mowed.

And dominating everything the lofty red cliffs, like towering guardians of a paradise that humans transgressed at their risk.

We were accompanied by the Trephina ranger, Paul Dahl, and a German-born Top End ranger, Frank Woerle. Frank, probably one of the Territory's best bushmen, has accumulated mountains of experience in his thirty-odd years of roaming the Territory's outback. But even he was suitably stunned by the spectacle. We camped late in the evening at a grassy slope against benign rocks weathered by time. Only a small rivulet of black but clear running water remained of the mighty Hale River that has carved the Ruby. But I imagined the colossal impact of a flood between those mighty walls. It must be a terrifying show.

As the evening wore on, the stars shone through the wide gap to give yet another dimension to the great enclosure that surrounded us. Barely distinguishable as dark marks in the night, the cliffs stood watch.

I was curious about the origins of the name Ruby. The ranger, Paul, informed us that in 1886 the explorer David Lindsay made his way along this part of the Hale and found what he thought were rubies. News of the find started a small 'ruby rush' and for a time about one hundred eager miners battled the heat, cold and extreme isolation in a feverish search.

After eighteen months their 'ruby fever' vanished when the red stones, which abound in the gorge's bed, were shown to be

garnets and almost worthless. The chance discovery of gold at Arltunga then offered new hope for a few penniless ruby miners.

Lindsay baptised the eastern part of Glen Annie Gorge after his wife, but it is really the same geological formation although at the end of it there are a number of much smaller tributary gorges and ravines in which it is easy to get lost. If you are going to walk the area make sure you can retrace your steps by leaving markers or get a good layout of the land behind you before you move forward.

The far eastern corner of the gorge is also marked by patches of whitewash on the cliffs where falcons and kestrels perch. In the river sands there are many tracks of dingoes and rock wallabies, and numerous, tiny, glassy red garnets.

Then comes one of the most moving parts of the visit. Paul told me about a lonely grave at the other end of the gorge and gave general indications how to find it. At the crack of first light I left the party for a longish walk to the east. There is a huge black dyke guarding the mouth of the gorge and, at its northern end, a sandy, rocky knoll. On top of the windswept knoll there is a bleak little grave with a headstone that reads: T. Ph. Fox died here at 55 years of age on 25 May 1888.

Who was that man? Thomas Phineas? Information provided by another ranger, Gerry O'Neill, is that he committed suicide. Why? What were his final thoughts as he gave up life? Why did he come here? Why did he finally despair and end it all in the midst of magnificent splendour?

Well past his prime, Fox died in one of the most majestic places human eyes can see. I am sure the gorge's cliffs were sympathetic.

PHOTOGRAPH BY NEIL PHILLIPS

The lonely headstone at Glen Annie Gorge.

One day this will become a major attraction for visitors. It is not just the gorge, but the surrounding countryside. Wild, magnetic and untamed. This is Central Australia at its very best. It is not going to be transformed overnight though. The road is difficult to negotiate and, undoubtedly, this will be a major factor restricting visitation.

I must point out however that getting lost in that environment could be most unpleasant. The normal precautions plus a good map and compass therefore apply.

137

An aerial view of Alice Springs at dawn.

PHOTOGRAPH BY CONSERVATION COMMISSION

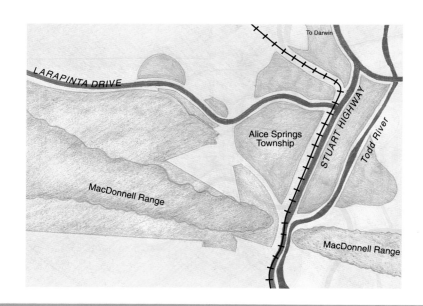

ALICE SPRINGS

I first read Neville Shute's *A Town Like Alice* in my native Spanish language and I fell in love with the girl at a distance. I saw the original film, too, and I thought I would not want to die without visiting this town and becoming acquainted with its people.

I was not disappointed. The Alice is everything I expected it to be and then some. It is a town with a heart, nestled in the Red Centre amidst the splendid Macdonnell Ranges, wrestling with its glorious past, but, at least in my view, curiously afraid of the present.

It is not an exuberant and brash town such as Darwin, where almost anything goes and is expected. Alice Springs is far more restrained and, dare one say it, much more elegant than Darwin. Here lives the true spirit of pioneers. This is an Australian town and makes absolutely no apologies for it.

Alice Springs was the product of high adventure and romance, and these live on. Like Darwin, the Alice owes her origins to the Overland Telegraph. The English astronomer Charles Todd, who had arrived in the colony of South Australia in 1855 at age 29 to supervise the SA Government's telegraph lines, was put in charge of the Overland Telegraph in 1871. He entrusted the construction of the line to five surveyors, R. R. Knuckey, G. R. McMinn, W. W. Mills, A. T. Woods and H. Harvey. All except Mills had been with Goyder in the original survey of Palmerston (Darwin) so they had good Territory experience.

A Territory historian, Professor Alan Powell, (in *Far Country*) puts the story that followed like this:

Men joined their parties eagerly, for the high pay and the lure of the unknown. The Scot, John Ross, bald, black-bearded and like his countryman Stuart, toughened by years of searching the remote corners of Australia for pastoral land, became explorer for the central teams, charged with finding a shorter route than Stuart's through the Centralian ranges. Young bushman Alfred Giles, dreaming of "undiscovered wealth, of great rivers, of bold mountain peaks … of new minerals … of wild savages", offered to join him. "Are you sound in mind and limb?" asked Ross. "Can you live on bandicoot and goanna?" Giles said he had already done so. "Then you'll do," said Ross. The surveyor Mills had the credit for discovering the Heavitree Gap, where the Todd River breaks through the Macdonnell Ranges, and the spring which he named Alice, after Todd's wife in March 1871.

The name stuck despite efforts to change it to Stuart, which is what the new settlement was to be officially called when established in 1883, following a rush of prospectors to a gemstone field in the Macdonnells. The field was thought to be rubies, but they were garnets. Still, miners in substantial numbers arrived and they camped under the gum trees in the Todd River, north of Heavitree Gap. That was the start of 'a town like Alice'.

Officially, it was called Stuart but, as in Darwin where the locals rejected the name 'Palmerston', its inhabitants insisted on Alice Springs and this was accepted by the Commonwealth in 1933 as the town's name.

As Powell explains, the town had a modest start. In 1889, Wally Benstead built the Stuart Arms Hotel and, five years later, there were three stores, a butcher and a few private houses. When an adventurous

An overview of the Overland Telegraph Station at Alice Springs. The buildings were designed to take summer's scorching heat and winter's freezing temperatures. They stand alone, away from the town itself, a stark reminder of the loneliness of the great Australian frontier.

PHOTOGRAPH BY WELDON TRANNIES

bicycle rider, J. J. Murif, came through in 1896, pedalling his bike on an epic ride through the continent from north to south, he called the settlement 'Sleepy Hollow … All shade and silence and tranquillity'.

Essentially, Alice Springs had two reasons to exist. One was to service the telegraph line and the Telegraph Station, now a major tourist attraction. The other was to service the surrounding cattle stations. Powell gives a sensitive account of the lives of women in the town and surrounds at the turn of the century:

> Restricted though their lives were, the white women of Alice Springs were not alone. For the very few who ventured with their men on to the remote cattle stations, fear was a constant companion—fear of accident or illness far from help, fear for the future of their children, fear of wild blacks …

In my travels through Centralia, I once came upon a charming stone cottage that had been abandoned. It was powerfully built and had a wide verandah overlooking a dry creek fringed by tall ghost gums. Inside, there were four bedrooms and a lounge room with a huge fireplace for the bitter winter nights. There, in the lounge room, was a piano, the only piece of furniture inside. I thought that the house had a story to tell but I did not know what it was. Perhaps it was the story of the terrible loneliness of a woman.

The Great Australian Loneliness is the Alice's heart and soul. The rail link from Port Augusta reached the tiny settlement in 1929 and assured its future. The first party of wide-eyed tourists arrived by train in 1930. In 1936 Ellis Banking set out to reach Ayers Rock by motorcycle and died of thirst. In 1939, the Alice had reached metropolis levels. About 950 people lived there.

The war brought big changes to Alice Springs, as it did to the rest of the Northern Territory. The first military convoy passed through the Alice on its way to Darwin in 1941. It was the harbinger of traffic that would see hundreds of thousands of troops moved north in a bid to first dissuade the Japanese from invading Australia, then to attack Japan's soft underbelly in South-East Asia. From March 1942, the whole Territory was put under military control and the civilian administration under Administrator Abbott transferred to Alice Springs which, effectively, became the

Territory's capital for the remaining years of the war. The Army deported more than 100 people from the Alice as 'undesirable' between May 1942 and September 1943, and the military authorities refused to allow public servants there to have their wives with them. The little town stopped being 'Sleepy Hollow' while the military machine thrashed about.

All the same, Alice Springs survived the effects of the war and occupation by thousands of soldiers a lot better than Darwin, which not only suffered from Japanese bombing but was looted and devastated by Australian and American soldiers. Even in the 1950s, Australia's Prime Minister Robert Menzies compared Darwin quite unfavourably with Alice Springs, and expressed the hope that one day the northern town would begin to look like its Central Australian kin.

That cannot be, of course, because the climate and geography are quite different. There are no easy definitions about either town, although it would be fair and accurate to say that Alice Springs has retained more character than Darwin, because there have not been the same interruptions in its development. There is continuity here, the most quintessential factor missing in Darwin's life. Also, arguably, the Alice is kinder and more genteel. Its hilly surroundings are more striking than Darwin's monotonous flatness and the architecture is influenced by the winter's cold when temperatures often drop to zero and below.

With 21 000 people, the Alice is just a small town. It is cosy and familiar, with great little restaurants and hotels. From here, it is an easy drive to superb holiday retreats, such as Glen Helen in the west or Ross River in the east. And for those who enjoy camping, there are dozens of destinations, each more beautiful than the other, from Trephina to Arltunga to Ruby Gorge in the east, to the Larapinta Trail in the west. The spirits of pioneers live here and they tell you that their efforts have not been in vain. This impossible town exists and, for me at any rate, it symbolises something unique in the Australian character—the will to build and create a good life from a harsh and hostile environment. I have not ever been in a more civilised town or one that better defines Australia.

Moody skies over the outskirts of Alice Springs.

PHOTOGRAPH BY GUNTHER DEICHMANN/WELDON TRANNIES

The pink cockatoo is often seen in grasslands and mulga country, especially near creekbeds. Its distinctive plumage and dramatic flight help make it a much photographed bird.

PHOTOGRAPH BY FRANK WOERLE

142

TREPHINA GORGE

About 85 kilometres east of Alice Springs is a charming nature park that should not be missed—Trephina Gorge. The park is accessible to all vehicles during the whole year.

Trephina is everything you did not want to risk your car, life or limb to see. It is a cosy gorge noted for its quartz cliffs and river red gum-lined watercourses.

One big surprise awaits the visitor here. The sunsets are arguably unequalled in the Territory. It may be the quartz on the walls or the rugged nature of the red rocks, but, whatever the reasons, sunsets here are exceptionally beautiful.

But the sunsets are not the only attraction at Trephina. The camping facilities are among the best of any Territory park. There are picnic areas located at Trephina Bluff and at a charming series of three waterholes, John Hayes Rockhole. Each of these areas has toilet facilities, including a disabled unit at the gorge, wood barbecues and picnic benches. Camping areas with tap water are situated at Trephina Gorge and Bluff.

The John Hayes Rockhole is a popular swimming location during the warmer months. Swimming, though, is not a particularly popular sport in winter anywhere in the Centre where temperatures often fall below zero. There are two walking tracks radiating from the holes. One is to a lookout providing views over the dissected creek. A longer walk, the Trephina Ridgetop Walk, is recommended for experienced and well equipped walkers only. The walk follows the ridge top and offers panoramic views of the surrounding region.

Four walks radiate from the carpark including the Ridgetop Walk through John Hayes Rockhole. The shorter Saltbush Walk takes in the south side of Trephina Bluff where the extremely rare Thozets box tree can be seen.

People planning overnight walks away from the camping ground should contact the ranger. And just take the normal precautions—hat, good footwear and, most importantly, **water**.

Most people prefer to visit the park during the cooler months of April to September. But the park, unless one wants to walk, is at its best after some heavy rains when thin rivulets from each of the hills flow slowly to the river below.

That is when the whole river system comes alive, bringing an awareness of the immense force of the water that has carved these marvellous gorges over the millennia.

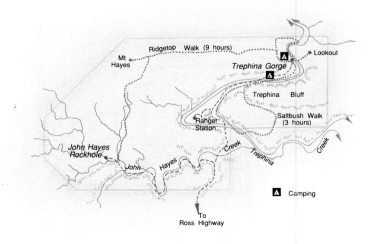

The Bush Tucker Man beside a mature ghost gum. This tree harbours edible grubs, and its bark was used by Aborigines to make dishes.

PHOTOGRAPH BY STEVE STRIKE

Trephina Gorge runs out of water during the Dry but it is possible to swim all year round at John Hayes Rockhole. Here, on a hot day the visitor can sit in the broken shade of old eucalypts and look out at the high rock walls glowing pink and ochre in the sunlight.

Southeast of Trephina is N'Dhala Gorge whose walls are decorated by rock carvings at least 20 000 years old. To the west is Corroboree Rock, of great significance to the Arrente Aborigines. The rock contains a hole, just like a giant eye of a needle, carved by a collapsed joint. This is where the Arrente lawmen used to keep their churingas (sacred totems usually made of wood or stone), but the site, because of European intrusion, is not in use any longer.

Finally, still in the East Macdonnells but close to Alice Springs, there are two well known little gorges, Emily Gap and Jessie Gap, named after the wives of early white explorers and surveyors. They both contain permanent water and were thus of enormous value to the Arunta.

The denizens of this world of broken rocky hills are fascinating little creatures who, if you care enough, will communicate with you and tell you all about their home and neighbourhood.

The cracks in the rock walls reveal the mud nests of fairy martins and wasps.

The abundance of fractured rock in the park makes it an ideal place for reptiles. There are, for example, tiny military dragons which try to frighten larger animals with their puffed up pomposity. They are all bluff but, since they have been getting away with it for perhaps millions of years, it must work. There are also two-metre-long perenties, inoffensive except for their awesome size. They all need the rocks because that is their abode when temperatures rise to the high forties in summer and plummet well below zero in winter.

In the pools themselves there are small dark pond snails that feed on algae preventing its growth from choking the pool. Grotesque but strangely graceful tadpoles and water beetles swim frenetically back and forth, always on the move.

The river red gums, so well and uniquely portrayed by Namatjira, ghost gums, whitewoods and ironwoods in the valley floors are decorated all year round with noisy and colourful birds. Port Lincoln parrots, mistletoe birds, western thrushes and cheeky pied butcher birds are just some that add their welcome songs to a scenery that suits a peaceful oasis where one can rest and relax and forget things like politics, stock exchanges and city traffic.

In the clean air above the mountains and ranging down the valley floor are the birds of prey—little falcons, goshawks and wedgetailed eagles, all looking for the sick, the lame and unwary. That is life.

Do not rush everywhere like a tourist doing 20 European capitals in two days. Just take your time. Sit on a rock under the shade and let a few minutes lapse for the

Trephina Gorge, 85 kilometres east of Alice Springs, can be reached easily in a conventional vehicle.

PHOTOGRAPH BY CONSERVATION COMMISSION

frightened little creatures to forget there is a human monster in their midst and resume their normal life. You will be surprised at the riot and cacophony that soon surrounds you.

Unfortunately there are some introduced animals that have done, and continue to do, much damage to the environment: rabbits, donkeys and cats. They are lovely animals but when one sees first hand the terrible damage they are doing to the native environment one cannot but regret their introduction. Unless controlled, by some fairly ruthless culling, we will have no environment to speak of in the next generation.

A final note about this well managed and well appointed park. It is smack bang in the East Macdonnell Ranges. Now, everybody enthuses about—and justifiably so—the West Macdonnells. I prefer the East Macs. I think it is the stupendous hues and the beautiful colours of the sunsets. Or it may be that I am still trying to recover from a visit to the most astonishing gorge I have ever seen—Ruby. But that is another story.

Trephina is a place to relax in almost perfect communion with nature.

The Central Ranges provide a changing array of vivid colour as the seasons pass.

PHOTOGRAPH BY CONSERVATION COMMISSION

146

WEST MACDONNELLS

West from Alice Springs are the Macdonnell Ranges, a giant broken landscape of red escarpments, low jagged mountains and shattered rocks.

It is indivisible. You cannot partition one piece from the other, separate one particular aspect from the whole. The West Macdonnells, West Macs as they are called by the locals, stand as a unity defying man to break what nature has wrought.

Driving on a sealed road the landscape unfolds itself, ever changing yet retaining a sameness that eventually dulls the senses and leads one to believe there may be disappointment after all in this appalling jumble of truncated hills and valleys.

Not so. For the West Macdonnell Ranges are part of a series of almost parallel ridges that stretch for 500 kilometres east-west of Alice Springs. They are the artery that makes the heart of Australia palpitate and vibrate with life. Around them is the calcified body of the most ancient land on earth. But here there is water. The Macdonnells are the reservoir of the centre. They are the catchment and hoarding area for scarce rain and humidity. They treasure the winter's hard frost and save spring's dew. And when the sun wreaks vengeance in summer, this range of low hills laughs

and provides precious water to the surrounding countryside.

The spectacular serrated landscape that unfolds in front of your eyes tells an epic story. These were huge mountains once, rising 5000 metres into the sky, lording over vast jungles and well watered plains. Erosion and weathering have made them what they are today—the gnarled and angry remnants of a colossus still fighting a lone and giant battle against the fierce sun and desert.

Central Australia has not seen good surface water for perhaps 25 000 years. But the Macdonnells protect the little there is with zeal. Its incomparable gorges and crevices, ravines and gullies, like the wrinkles of Old Man Mountain, are the dams and reservoirs that nature chose to build so that the centre would not die.

There is a sealed road at the base of the range leading to a charming inn, the Glen Helen Lodge. The inn looks at a stretch of sandy beach nestling against the backdrop of a magnificent gorge of the same name. The gorge is owned and managed by the Conservation Commission.

The lodge is in fact an old homestead beautifully restored after a fire destroyed the original buildings. It is part and parcel

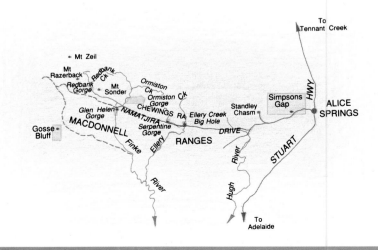

Impressions of a lunar landscape, West Macdonnells.

The Centralian blue-tongued lizard, found throughout most of the Northern Territory as well as in parts of Western Australia and eastern Queensland.

PHOTOGRAPH BY FRANK WOERLE

of the great pioneering traditions that opened up Central Australia. One of those pioneers, a top stockman and true blue Territorian, Bryan Bowman, has written a short history of the place, *The Glen Helen Story,* which is enthralling.

Some visitors make Glen Helen the base from which to explore one of the most spellbinding regions in the Territory. The setting is charming, hospitality warm and the meals delicious. Rooms are modest but clean and comfortable.

Many, however, prefer to 'rough it' in the various camping grounds in the area. The Conservation Commission maintains an information centre near the Ormiston Gorge which will give you all the details you need to set up a temporary base.

Swimming at the Glen is great, at least during the summer months. The water belongs to the mighty Finke River which is squeezed between the gorge's walls as it begins its epic journey to the Simpson Desert.

Although the whole of the West Macdonnells is spectacular, three places probably outshine the rest. They are Serpentine Gorge, Redbank Gorge and the Ormiston Gorge and Pound National Park. And this is just the beginning for a region that has so much to offer that any detailed description would demand a book on its own.

The Serpentine and Redbank gorges are in some ways similar. Both are nature's work of art with steep, high rising walls almost touching each other in places. They give the impression they stand guard, proud of the remarkable beauty within and awesome in their silence.

After the flood of Easter 1988 the Redbank lost its icy waters for a time and was dry when I visited it. I walked the whole length stopping every so often to gaze in total awe at the cliffs rising about 100 metres up and away from sight. Higher than the extended arm could reach they had been burnished and polished by the waters, their colours

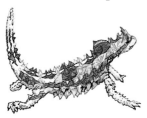

The majestic Mount Sonder, a portion of the West Macdonnell Ranges.

PHOTOGRAPH BY FRANK WOERLE

151

running the gamut from pure black to red and white.

The feeling was that of walking into an immense cave with a blue slit for a ceiling. The blue was deep azure, much more appropriate in a gemstone than in the sky. A Canadian walker commented he had never seen skies as blue as in Central Australia and said that, on his return home, he would find it impossible to express in simple words the colour of the sky. Perhaps the works of that great Aboriginal painter, Albert Namatjira, best reflect the pale azure intensity of that sky. It should be called the Namatjira blue.

Despite the friendly sky, however, the feeling persists that these walls, proud and huge, bulging with authority, have been put there to stand watch over a fortress millions of years old.

The allure of this fabulous gorge, carved to perfection over the ages, defies description. It must be seen and felt.

The approach is through a dry river bed, very easy walking on soft sand and some rock hopping. Sturdy footwear is recommended.

In contrast to Redbank, there was water in the Serpentine, plenty of it and very cold. Furthermore, at the very start of the walk to the gorge, there is a fairly deep waterhole which has to be waded and swum through on occasions if one wants to see the gorge. It is not difficult but, although this was the beginning of summer, the water was freezing. An inflatable airbed is probably the solution for the less adventurous.

The Serpentine is a uniquely attractive gorge with all the attributes of Redbank plus a great deal of clear water at the canyon end. You can have a refreshing swim here provided you take the normal precautions.

Ormiston is quite different. It is divided into the gorge and the fascinating Pound. The gorge, like all the others in this region, is absolutely spectacular. Here it is possible to swim at leisure in waters that have known the kiss of the sun instead of the eternal shadows of tall cliffs. This is a grand gorge, a gorge that offers pleasurable hospitality as well as an awe-inspiring experience. It is welcoming and embraces the visitor in friendship after the rather intimidating majesty of Redbank and Serpentine.

Do not be totally confident, however. It may be that the gorge is lying. For Ormiston is a deep passage carved through quartz revealing a remarkably complex folding that the gorge has exposed. The folding is unlikely to have come about just as a result of simple erosion. Something more, some colossal and only dimly understood forces, were at work here some millions of years ago to shape this tongue emanating from the Pound.

But the best part of Ormiston, at least in my view, are the various bushwalks organised for just about everyone, from middle-aged bourgeois suburbanites to energetic youngsters. Many a pleasurable hour can be spent walking this rugged terrain. The scenery, as is the case with all of the West Macdonnells, is breathtaking.

Then it is back to the camping grounds for a well-earned beer or two and the sizzle of steak and sausages on the fire.

A huge park is proposed stretching westward from Alice Springs some 160 kilometres along the Macdonnell Ranges to the remote and splendid Mount Zeil. The area is so scenic that the proposal makes eminent sense, not just from the conservation viewpoint but from sheer economics.

This will be a park rivalling Kakadu or Uluru and will include all that is best in Centralia. The ranges rise dramatically from the Central Australian arid lands. With their steep, red-faced slopes, they present outstanding scenery. They are also the habitat for endemic and rare animals and plants, some species of which have disappeared from elsewhere in Australia. Its management should be integrated.

One of the principal features in the new park is the magnificent Larapinta Trail, which meanders east-west for more than 220 kilometres.

Now, here is a challenge to bushwalkers from all over the world. The Larapinta Trail makes the most of the Macdonnells'

Vegetation struggles to exist in the rock wall of Redbank Gorge.

A pair of
tawny
frogmouths,
experts in the art
of camouflage.
When disturbed,
the tawny
frogmouth adopts
a 'broken branch'
posture, an
illusion made
complete by the
colour and
formation of its
plumage.

PHOTOGRAPH BY NEIL PHILLIPS

rmiston Gorge provides many bushwalks through the complex folding of its granite walls.

PHOTOGRAPH BY FRANK WOERLE

startling scenery providing access to a series of permanent and semi-permanent waterholes. Links for vehicle access is provided at several locations to allow walkers various options, from relatively short walks to the whole length of the Trail.

A portion of the Trail follows Stuart's original route through the Macdonnells. The Scot was the first European to feast his eyes on the wonder that is the Macdonnells, which he named after South Australian Governor, Sir Richard Macdonnell.

Let me make an easy prediction. The Larapinta Trail will become one of the world's great bushwalking adventures, attracting backpackers from around the world.

The Trail has been developed into stages of about twenty kilometres average although some, like the walk from Jay Creek to Standley Chasm, are shorter because they are steeper and more rugged.

I was very fortunate to walk part of the Trail with an old friend, Harry Butler, whose encyclopaedic knowledge of the bush is as astonishing as it is precious. It was he who explained to me some of the enduring remnants of Aboriginal presence here.

The Trail crosses the tribal lands of the Arrente who have lived here for many thousands of years. They chose this area because here there is water saved in crevices and impossibly beautiful ponds which sustained plants and animals, thus allowing the Aboriginal population to increase to relatively dense levels.

Incredibly, Aboriginal traditions faithfully reflect the geological history of the region. They say that the dawn of time broke over a flat, featureless earth inhabited by powerful spirit beings that took the shape of plants, animals and people. They were the ancestors of all life and Aborigines believe that their power lives on in the landscape that they created. It does, and they will look after visitors but not if they do silly things, for this is dangerous country and should not be taken lightly.

Please heed the warnings of experienced rangers. First, climate. There are extremes of temperatures. This may mean closing the Trail between the months of October to March because it will be too hot for walkers. Waterholes are few and far between and it takes only a a short time to dehydrate and die.

Second, safety. Distances will make communication a difficult problem to overcome, particularly where injuries are concerned.

Third, water. Remember, there is virtually no water west of Bowman's Gap. Walkers may have to carry 2-3 days supply of water in the more remote sections of the Trail.

Whether summer or winter, make sure you have sturdy footwear, a hat, and that you do not roam out into the yonder without letting the ranger know precisely where you intend to go. Remember, common sense saves lives, including your own.

A young Aboriginal girl enjoys the sweet nectar from the honey grevillea, a popular bush food.

PHOTOGRAPH BY DEREK ROFF

The red cabbage palms common to Palm Valley exist nowhere else in the world, and have survived here for at least 10 000 years—'plant dinosaurs' from a prehistoric age.

PHOTOGRAPH BY DEREK ROFF

FINKE GORGE

The 46 000 hectare Finke Gorge National Park, south-west of Alice Springs, is more popularly known as Palm Valley, the home of the rare red cabbage palm.

There are some 3000 or so of these palms here and they exist nowhere else in the world. A miracle? It most certainly is. The graceful palms have survived at least 20 000 years, possibly longer, and their genes in all likelihood stretch to the age of the great reptiles that roamed the jungles here when Australia was Gondwanaland, a hunk of the earth's crust drifting away from Africa.

These seemingly fragile plants, slender and vulnerable under the scorching sun, have survived as the only living testimony of another era when Central Australia was a vast rainforest populated by a myriad birds, reptiles (including of course the ubiquitous crocodile) and numerous other animals that disappeared after a mysterious climatic change some 20–25 000 years ago.

The change made this region one of the most arid and inhospitable on earth. It killed the jungle the birds and the animals and sent the crocodiles scurrying to the more benign northern waters. Nothing survived—except these rare and exquisitely beautiful tropical palms in a most untropical environment (winter temperatures in Central Australia fall well below zero and the palms are as far away from the influence of the sea as they can be). Why did this little corner survive untouched over the millennia? No one knows with any certainty. Perhaps the gorge carved by the Finke River protected it. Maybe the Aborigines here did not develop a taste, as they did in the north, for its fibrous stem which, when cut, of course kills the plant. All we know is that the palms exist and, perhaps, that ought to be enough for they are a grand sight.

Nor is that the end of the story. Palms need water, plenty of it, to survive. That is why they grow in profussion along tropical coasts with predictable and abundant rainfall. But there is no water here except what is provided by the seepage from the Finke River and from the gorge's forbidding rocks.

And the palms are not alone, for the park contains about 400 plant types of which 30 are extremely rare, the remnants of another era that has disappeared everywhere else but, for some mysterious reason, not here.

Your appetite not yet whetted? Okay, toss in now spectacular scenery, views that will evoke vivid images of some as yet undiscovered planet, good camping grounds

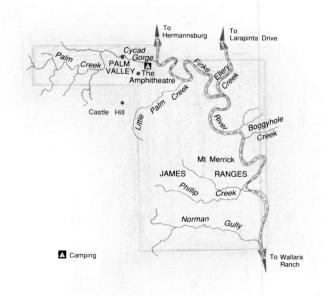

served by tap water, fantastic opportunities for photography and great bushwalks. I suggest you climb the Amphitheatre for some of the most incredible views you are likely to see anywhere, or walk to the Cycad Gorge, named after the extremely rare and old Macrozamia cycad, another remnant of the original forests. You now have a fair picture of the Finke Gorge Park, an almost unbelievable combination of living geography and rare botany.

But perhaps you are more taken by anthropology and history than you are by botany or geography. In that case you may be interested to know that Finke and the surrounding area contain locations of significant cultural value to Aborigines as well as evidence of early European settlement.

The palms were first noticed by the explorer Ernest Giles in 1872. The Old Boggy Hole Police Depot, inside the park, and the township of Hermannsburg, outside, provide evidence of early European settlement. Indeed Hermannsburg is the site for some fine early mission churches built by Lutheran German missionaries in 1877.

The famous Aboriginal painter, Albert Namatjira, grew up here. His cottage, well preserved on the side of the road to Finke, should be of interest to visitors.

The course of the Finke River traditionally formed a major trade and travel route for central ranges and western desert Aborigines, and is one of the oldest watercourses in the world.

It is a place you may want to explore at leisure for a few days or, for the more curious, perhaps for weeks or months. For Finke is a precious relic of times gone by that cannot be found anywhere else.

The Commission advises that the park is accessible all year round except on rare occasions when the river is in flood. The cooler months from April to September are the most pleasant months to visit (bearing in mind that night temperatures can fall below freezing). Summer temperatures often reach the mid-forties or even higher and can make your visit distinctly uncomfortable, particularly if you have not taken sensible precautions like wearing a hat and a shirt and carrying water.

If you intend to take a walk further from the valley itself, make sure you tell the ranger.

The park is strictly for four-wheel drive vehicles. The 13 kilometre road from

The death adder attracts prey through deception. By partially burying itself and moving the very tip of its tail, it attracts interested predators.

PHOTOGRAPH BY FRANK WOERLE

Ancient weathered rock formations at Finke Gorge.

PHOTOGRAPH BY FRANK WOERLE

Hermannsburg is rock-strewn and the sandy river bed makes driving difficult but the reward is well worth it.

The gorge is a delight. The red terraced walls contrast sharply with the river bed, paved with old grey rocks. Initiation Rock, a large outcrop in the Amphitheatre where Arrente boys were initiated into manhood, provides a perfect viewing platform for the most breathtaking scenery. The river, meandering pale and ghostly between the walls, provides a little water to red gums often draped in beautiful but deadly mistletoe.

It is peaceful here and, so far, relatively untouched country. But this won't last. Palm Valley is a precious jewel that people from all over the world will want to see.

Gosse Bluff is a crater five kilometres wide, believed to have been formed by the impact of a meteorite which shook the earth.

PHOTOGRAPH BY FRANK WOERLE

GOSSE BLUFF

HENBURY METEORITES

 n the way from the West Macdonnell Ranges to Hermannsburg and Finke Gorge is Gosse Bluff.

The Bluff is the place where the history of earth changed. What you will see here does not exist anywhere else in the world—a vast crater formed when an object from outer space collided with earth with an unimaginable impact.

Other craters, mute witnesses of meteorites, do exist around the world. But none like Gosse Bluff.

For here the impact did not just depress the ground, it did not just make a large hole, it created a huge outer wall around a pulverised, crushed landscape.

No one knows with any certainty what the object was. It could have been a giant meteor, an asteroid or, more likely, a rogue comet. Scientists have called it a bolide. It hurtled unannounced towards the earth, perhaps 130 million years ago, and hit with an estimated force at least 200 000 times greater than the nuclear explosion that destroyed Hiroshima.

The colossal detonation created an immense mushroom cloud that rose thousands of metres into the atmosphere. Below nothing, absolutely nothing, remained except the convulsed red hot rocks wrenched from depths of two or three kilometres to a ghastly surface they had never been meant to see. They stand in solitary testimony to one of the most cataclysmic episodes in the history of mother earth.

For thousands of square kilometres there was utter devastation. Not a single living thing remained to tell the awful story. Not a plant, not an animal, nothing. The mushroom cloud spread, bringing the inevitable cooling of the earth's atmosphere and phenomenal climatic changes around the world.

It is not at all beyond credulity that such a massive collision caused the earth to wobble or shudder. Huge tidal waves, cyclonic winds, savage earthquakes and volcanoes would have followed. In the end, planet earth settled back on its serene course in the solar system, but it was not the same planet. Vast changes in the genetic composition of plants and animals must have occurred. Maybe, just maybe, this is the time when the seed of mammals was planted. A few million years later, at the end of the Mesozoic era some 65 million years ago, they were to replace the huge reptiles that had existed when the bolide hit the flat lands of Central Australia.

Gosse Bluff is therefore not a bluff in the true sense of the word, but the relic of an awesome clash between the earth and an extraterrestrial object, probably a comet. If viewed from a good distance, the observer will see a large, 20 to 25 kilometres, circular depression, in effect Gosse's outer crater. It is a spectacle that grips the mind.

There is a four-wheel drive track that leads into the huge five kilometre-wide inner crater. Stand in the middle, look at the 200 metre walls surrounding you and

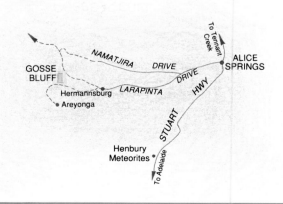

imagine this huge bolide moving silently through space on a collision course with this precise spot.

The Aborigines believe this is a sacred site, a place that once saw great evil. They are of course correct. Astronomers tell us, however, that large comets or meteorites the size of the one that caused Gosse Bluff only strike the earth once in thousands or millions of years.

Does this mean we are overdue for another hit?

Gosse Bluff was discovered by the explorer Ernest Giles in 1872 but he thought it was just another stunted range of red hills. Giles named the range after a good friend, Harry Gosse, and went on to the West Macdonnells blissfully unaware he had been the first European to sight the most terrifying testimony of earth's fragility.

It was not until the 1960s in fact that Gosse Bluff was identified as the site of a bolide impact. The United States' Gemini 5 spacecraft took some pictures that left little room for doubt. The Bluff could only have been formed by a huge explosion, probably by an object from outer space.

This was confirmed by a team of academics from the Australian National University. Gosse Bluff has since become a place of interest not only for curious tourists, but for its deep scientific value.

Aborigines came upon the idea of a huge collision with an extra-terrestrial object much earlier than European Australians. In Arrente tradition the Bluff was created after a vast wooden dish used as a baby carrier crashed to earth during Creation.

Gosse Bluff is a registered Aboriginal sacred site and was handed over to the traditional Western Arrente owners by the Northern Territory Government in 1990 under Territory freehold title. In turn, the Arrente agreed to lease back the area to the Conservation Commission to be managed as a park under joint management.

At least 29 species of bird have been recorded here although information about the fauna is still very scanty. About five rare plants are also found at the Bluff including a stand of the Western Desert Grass-tree.

Access into this unique feature is by four-wheel drive vehicle only, and camping is restricted to the Ipolera campground, about 20 kilometres to the south.

Of course if natural phenomena are of particular interest to you, there is another fascinating little place in the Northern Territory that you should not miss. It is the Henbury Meteorite Craters, a small conservation reserve about 147 kilometres south-east of Alice Springs, with easy access by conventional vehicle from the Stuart Highway.

The site consists of twelve craters formed several thousand years ago when a falling meteorite broke into fragments and struck the ground.

The largest crater is 180 metres wide and 15 metres deep while the smallest is barely recognisable at six metres wide and only a few centimetres deep.

Picture yourself on a quiet, clear night in Central Australia several thousand years ago. From the sky comes a blinding trail of light. Giant fires plummet downward and the countryside is lit for hundreds of kilometres. The fires smash into the ground with a noise many times greater than the loudest crack following a close lightning strike. Twisted rocks and pieces of iron fly through the sky like giant and deadly shrapnel.

Darkness returns quite suddenly as shockwaves bounce and rumble through the ground. In seconds it is over, leaving clouds of dust, a faint smell of burnt metal and twelve gaping holes in the ground.

Today, we know that it was a meteorite that shattered and blazed a fiery path through our planet's atmosphere until its pieces crashed into the earth here.

Whether local Aborigines witnessed this spectacle and what they made of it is not known. However, significantly, this place is known to them as 'sun walk fire devil rock'.

The Henbury meteorite began as a fast moving mass of metal which plunged into the earth's atmosphere.

How big was the piece that caused the largest crater? Probably no bigger than a fuel drum, but enough to wreak awesome destruction. Like Gosse Bluff, the Henbury meteorite site is yet another example of natural forces that we barely understand.

The needle-like leaves of the grass-tree provide a smaller surface for the sun to shine on—an important adaptive mechanism enabling the plant to cope with extreme heat.

PHOTOGRAPH BY FRANK WOERLE

The towering red cliffs of Kings Canyon stand more than 100 metres above the valley which Kings Creek follows.

PHOTOGRAPH BY FRANK WOERLE

166

KINGS CANYON

Kings Canyon, about 310 kilometres southwest of Alice Springs, is the most striking feature in the Watarrka National Park which includes basically the whole of the George Gill Range.

The canyon itself is an angry cut on the range. The 200 metre sandstone walls have been sliced so neatly they appear a work of engineering rather than nature. The result is a splendid canyon topped by rock domes and carvings formed by the combined action of wind and water.

At the bottom there is lush vegetation hiding huge boulders chaotically tossed and pitched in total disarray. There is no rhyme or reason about the gigantic slabs in the creek bed. They have been put there by a cataclysm of gigantic proportions leaving only the sheer walls to remind the observer that there is, after all, order in nature.

The canyon's dominating features are of course its northern and southern walls. They are twins and share striking similarities. Both are sheer and commanding, tall, proud and impressive.

But they are also very different. The north wall is smooth and shines like red glass. Its northern sister is pocked and brown, uglier perhaps, but spectacular nevertheless. They complement each other, speaking of a time when they belonged deep in the earth's womb and were still united by the continuity of sandstone.

For this canyon has not been formed by the slow work of water. It is the product of a sudden and massive eruption, a seismic revolution, a geological debacle.

There is nothing gentle about it. Kings Canyon is not a 'nice' canyon offering tame sights or soft views. It explodes with unbelievable energy. It is powerful, awesome, insolent in the knowledge that it was born to rule. It makes the wind talk. It holds the rain and the sun in contempt. This canyon is king.

Yet it is no despot, for it harbours some beautiful and delicate vegetation that, without the canyon's protection, would have undoubtedly died off.

Here lives a rare cycad that takes the observer to bygone ages along with acacia trees and fragile palms. Indeed the Aboriginal name for the acacias, Watarrka, is the park's name. This is one of the most important botanic areas in Central Australia. Some 750 plant species have already been identified within the park's boundaries, among them several extremely rare and relict species including ferns that proliferate at the bottom of Kings Canyon. You can feast your eyes on one of the most priceless gifts anyone can have: touching or seeing something that relatively few humans have seen or touched. Something that does not exist elsewhere and that is fragile and of exquisite beauty.

Nor are the impressive walls and unique vegetation the end of this fascinating feature. Kings Canyon has more surprises in store. The plateau-like summit is a

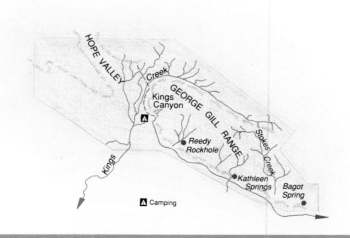

K̲ings Canyon contains several rare and relict plant species—plants from a bygone geological era, like these cycads.

PHOTOGRAPH BY FRANK WOERLE

The knob-tailed gecko is nocturnal and feeds on arthropods and smaller lizards. The purpose of its knob is unknown.

PHOTOGRAPH BY TED SANDERY

wonderland of turrets, domes and temples that transport you into a metropolis that has disappeared. The Lost City is what its name indicates—the ruins of an ancient city shaped by formidable geological forces to give it the appearance of a long-lost urban centre stretching over a very large area.

The summit can be reached after a steep climb which, in summer, can be very arduous. Hat, sturdy footwear and, above all, a good supply of water are a must. The return walk is only about six kilometres but it takes an average of about three to four hours. The terrain is very rugged and can be exhausting and difficult.

But once on top the views are truly astonishing. The Lost City is a park within a park. You turn enchanting corners only to be confronted with more of the same. The rim is not fenced. That means you must remain on the marked track because there could be danger if you depart from it and take unnecessary risks.

Eventually you climb down to a hidden paradise on the head of the canyon. Now you are on the open summit, suddenly you enter a crevice, a corridor almost, that opens into an amphitheatre of stunning beauty. You have arrived at the aptly named Garden of Eden.

This is a chain of pools fringed by cycads protected by high walls. Here you can forget that there is a world outside. It cannot be natural. This surely must have been a marvellous garden constructed by a monarch for his lover. The two would come here and spend hours or perhaps days away from prying eyes in the most incredible luxury.

The sough of a gentle breeze barely stirs

the ancient cycads. To the west of the enclosure are only the twin walls of the canyon. Below is a tangled mass of vegetation and broken boulders. Behind is the protecting crevice. Beside are pools, ferns and cycads. Above is the Central Australian sky.

Two more things should be added here. The first, is that the Watarrka (Kings Canyon) National Park is of special significance to the Luritja people who are involved in the Park's management through a local management committee.

The second, is that Aboriginal involvement also includes a joint venture in the establishment of the Kings Canyon Wilderness Lodge, a marvellous example of what can and should be done to promote tourism without breaking the quintessential character of the area. The Lodge blends beautifully with the landscape and indeed it is part of it.

But visitors should have at least some understanding of Aboriginal culture to appreciate the area because here at Watarrka, the Luritja provide the real thing, not some dusty study of obscure anthropological value in a museum.

The term Luritja really embraces all the people who speak Western Desert languages and for many thousands of years lived in this area. They comprise mainly Yankuntjantjara, Pitjantjatjara (who extend down to South Australia) and a small group of Martutjara.

The essence of their culture and the one word that brings them together is tjukurpa. It has been interpreted as meaning "Dreaming" but this is totally inadequate. Tjukurpa is everything. It explains the relationship between Creation and all the things that happened afterwards, including the present. It gives the Luritja a sense of order and predictability in their every day living, and is also the law that allows them to travel great distances in the desert without getting lost. Tjukurpa relates

The black-footed rock wallaby finds shelter and protection from predators by making rocky hillsides its home.

PHOTOGRAPH BY CONSERVATION COMMISSION

places, rocky outcrops, sandy creek beds, rock holes and small clumps of bushes to each other and to the people. They are in a real sense landmarks and that is why Aborigines do not need maps, compasses and protractors or satellite navigation aids to know where they are.

Astonishingly, tjukurpa has survived intact the intrusion of European civilisation which started with the first explorer, Ernest Giles, in 1872 and continued with the expansion of pastoralism. The clash between pastoralists and Aborigines here repeated the pattern elsewhere. There were plenty of killings and enormous disruption to Aboriginal society.

But the Luritja are now back at Watarrka. The people have survived and, just as important, their traditions and tenacious culture have also survived and this makes the Park a living thing, a very precious and rare gem.

Kings Canyon is more than a park, it is an unforgettable experience.

171

The colour of Ayers Rock is a result of the creation of iron oxides on its surface, brought about by the effects of air and moisture on some of the minerals in the rock itself.

PHOTOGRAPH BY DEREK ROFF

ULURU NATIONAL PARK

(AYERS ROCK & THE OLGAS)

*U*luru, giant rock, is the Aboriginal name for Ayers Rock, probably Australia's best recognised landmark. It is also the name of the park that includes Katatjuta, the Olgas. Yulara, on the other hand, which many visitors confuse for the park, is the large and distinctive resort outside the park's boundaries.

The Rock is the lord and master of the surrounding landscape. Most or all visitors have seen photographs, illustrations or television footage of Ayers Rock before they come. But nothing has prepared them for the physical impact of the vast monolith. Its sheer immensity dwarfs everything around, even the desert. Three hundred and thirty-five metres high and two and a half kilometres long … it stands alone in sumptuous glory.

What you are seeing here is nature's 40-million-year work of art. The Rock has not changed in that time. It and the Olgas are the relics of an immense bed of sedimentary rock now almost entirely covered by debris from erosion and by wind-blown sand. The 36 individual domes at the Olgas may once have been a single dome many times the size of Ayers Rock.

Once, many millions of years ago, this was the sea and the Rock an island. It is difficult not to think of it as an island today when the sea has gone and all that remains is the smooth rounded mammoth surrounded by flat arid lands.

The Rock can be climbed at its northwestern end. Indeed the climb appears to be an irresistible challenge to visitors who flock to the foot in the hope of an easy lark. There is nothing easy about the climb and no one should be under any misapprehension. You really are climbing the tip of an unimaginably large monolith, the mother and father of all rocks, that has survived millions of years of erosion and weathering. It is not going to surrender without a stiff fight.

The ascent is difficult and people with heart or respiratory problems or with a fear of heights should not attempt it. Once on top, however, the view is stunning. To the south are the barely distinguishable blue forms of the Petermann and Musgrave ranges. Lake Amadeus, named after a Spanish king, shimmers in the north. To the west are the majestic Olgas. Everywhere are the vast spinifex plains.

But Ayers Rock has acquired its awesome reputation not just because it is such an unbelievably unique landform. Its secret is

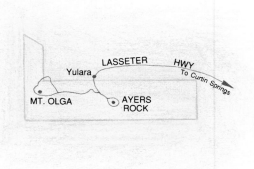

The changing faces of Ayers Rock:

Torrential rain creates rivers rushing down the sides of the Rock.
Following the storm the Rock is shrouded in a magnificent rainbow.
Freezing overnight temperatures leave a layer of frost over the Rock.
A dust storm erases the sun and engulfs the monolith.

PHOTOGRAPHS BY DEREK ROFF

that it can capture the sun and make it play the most alluring and enchanting games on its surface.

Sunrises and sunsets take on a brand new meaning on the Rock. Colours acquire shades and tones impossible to repeat on canvas. The sky, earth, clouds and sparse vegetation all change and become living things. They breathe and talk and sing. The stage is an amazing combination of constantly changing full dress rehearsals. And there is no finale for, when one thinks the show is over, it is instead a new beginning.

It is as enthralling a spectacle as you are likely to see anywhere.

From there to the Olgas is only 32 kilometres, but be warned about the road which is very rough indeed.

The Olgas, however, are worth the trip. They are a vast collection of tall domes forever challenging Ayers Rock for supremacy over the majestic landscape.

Again, nowhere on earth does anything similar exist. Some 36 massive monoliths, some much taller than the Rock itself, tower haughtily in an awesome display of geological arrogance. The story they tell is as old as the earth. It is one that springs from the bottom of lifeless seas helped by the fires beneath the crust and eventually emerges triumphant into the clean air on top. It survives millions of years of geological change. Their arrogance is therefore understandable.

And their withered beauty is breathtaking. Like the Rock, they too have acquired the magic powers to capture the sun and taught it to play countless tricks. Those are, if anything, even more spectacular than at the Rock. The reason is that the Olgas is the home of gorges and huge crevices which add incredible variety to the display of hues and colours.

But, at least in my view, the grand monoliths are at their best when rare but fierce desert storms hit. The sights then are indelible.

Immense black clouds slowly approaching until they cover the whole sky. They are not your mild, temperate region variety. These are thick, solid masses that can be touched and felt. They come with a regal paraphernalia of lightning and thunder, sparks and rumbling noise interrupted only by occasional shrill cracks when a bolt hits a stately desert oak.

The Olgas preen and rise to the challenge like medieval knights readying for a joust. The clouds, heralded by cool winds, issue the challenge. They roar defiance as they rush the huge domes and, suddenly, there are sheets of water mixed with the smell of sand, sizzling rocks and the sound of liquid.

The Olgas take the lash of wind and rain with contemptuous equanimity. They look like wraiths totally enveloped by dark clouds that, little by little, spend themselves in their futile attack and retreat to fight another day.

The Canberra-based organisation, the Australian National Parks and Wildlife Service (ANPWS), administers Uluru on behalf of the traditional Aboriginal owners, the Pitjantjatjara and Yankuntjantjara people, some of whom live in the Mutitjulu community at the foot of the Rock.

A pamphlet distributed by the ANPWS explains that Aboriginal people have lived in the Uluru area for at least 10 000 years. In 1872 and 1873 two explorers, Ernest Giles and W. E. Gosse, came through the area. They were followed by prospectors, dingo hunters and missionaries. Large sheep and cattle stations were established in what had previously been the exclusive preserve of Aborigines.

Again according to the pamphlet, grazing depleted bush food resources. During the severe droughts in the 1930s and 1950s, Aboriginal people were drawn into missions, cattle stations and government settlements by curiosity and the prospect of a reliable food supply.

But the Aborigines, Anangu in their language, continued their traditional ways, visiting kin in their ancestral lands, returning to bush foods, arranging and attending ceremonies and teaching young people the skills and beliefs that had always been essential for their survival.

On 26 October 1985 they won title to

During a good season in Central Australia dingoes generally eat rabbits, rodents and lizards. But during droughts they tend to prey more upon cattle (in small numbers) or, more often, red kangaroo.

Uluru and remain the traditional owners of the park. The Northern Territory government argued against the handover and, as the result of the dispute, the Aborigines decided to agree to ANPWS management rather than the Conservation Commission that had previously administered Uluru. The park, therefore, like Kakadu, remains a source of political controversy as well as a natural wonder.

The flora and fauna here are well worth seeing but you may have to be patient because, please remember, this is the desert and animals and plants often hide or disguise themselves in order to survive.

So far 150 different kinds of birds, 22 mammals, many reptiles and frogs, and nearly 400 plant species have been recorded in the park area. But, as the ANPWS explains, visitors are likely to see only a few of these. However, those who take their time on tracks and lookouts will be rewarded by seeing fascinating dryland plants and animals which actually cope with this forbidding environment.

Finally, it is impossible to close comment on Uluru without mentioning Yulara, the massive resort built by the NT government to serve the park.

Yulara was the dream of a former Territory Chief Minister, Paul Everingham, who against advice from many sources and the judgment of people who thought they knew better, decided in 1981 to proceed with a $150 million tourist resort, some 450 kilometres west of Alice Springs in the middle of the desert. The fact that in those days the road to the park was a dirt track and that there were no amenities or facilities for the large workforce that would have to be employed on site did not deter Everingham.

The resort became a reality and has won several architectural prizes as well as tourism awards. It is world class and an undeniable success, a testimony to what a little courage and imagination can achieve.

Worth noting in this context is that

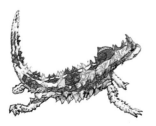

camping and picnicking are not permitted within the park but Yulara has excellent facilities not just for the upper end of the market but for tourists on more limited budgets.

The ANPWS has declared some places of significance to Aborigines out of bounds for visitors in both Ayers Rock and the Olgas. The restrictions must be observed.

Finally, I should mention a geographical form, Mount Conner, that many visitors confuse for Ayers Rock as they approach this well known landmark.

Mount Conner is a table-topped mountain about 100 kilometres east of the Rock. This is Artila for the Aborigines, the place where Ice Men created the cold. They could be correct for the area around Mount Conner

PHOTOGRAPH BY DEREK ROFF

The massive monoliths that are the Olgas rear proudly to the sky.

shows plenty of signs of a glacial age.

For some reason this particular feature has failed to attract the attention of its better known sisters to the west. Yet, Mount Conner is fascinating in itself.

It is a massive shape five kilometres long and two kilometres wide rising about 250 metres above the plains. There are literally dozens of caves at the base, some extending 40 metres into the rock. The whole thing is criss-crossed by marvellous gorges which provide access to the summit and spectacular views of the surrounding countryside.

Although Mount Conner is outside Uluru's boundaries it is really part of its unique landscape and should not be missed.

The sandstone walls of Chambers Pillar tower 50 metres above the surrounding plain. Its prominence made the pillar a guidepost for settlers travelling north, and evidence of their passing can still be seen in the soft sandstone.

PHOTOGRAPH BY DEREK ROFF

CHAMBERS PILLAR

(EWANINGA ROCKS & RAINBOW VALLEY)

I was curious about the type of country John McDouall Stuart had encountered when he entered the Northern Territory in his epic south-north crossing of Australia.

I decided on a quick visit to Chambers Pillar, an imposing monument in the desert that he named in honour of his mentor, James Chambers.

There may be directional problems for visitors wanting to re-create this fascinating episode in our history. I asked at the Erldunda pub and a young stockman told us to head towards Maryvale Station, about 100 kilometres east of the Stuart Highway, and then south to the Pillar.

The instructions proved accurate. Just follow the Stuart Highway until it intersects with the Hugh River stock route which leads to Maryvale. Then it is a hop and step away to Chambers Pillar.

We proceeded along immense and surprisingly lush plains hardly broken by elevations or hills. There were plenty of fat cattle around that stared at our car with rather uncaring and indifferent eyes until we came upon an old line.

Visitors, please be aware. If you are reading a map it may feature the abandoned railway as the real one. This may confuse you because in fact the line was moved a few kilometres to the west recently. After you reach the old line the track turns south about 50 kilometres to Maryvale.

The landscape becomes somewhat more rugged, but still easily negotiable, after Maryvale, a sprawling and well appointed station. Then, as the track crosses the highest point of the Charlotte Ranges, Chambers Pillar appears in the distance like the ultimate symbol of liberated manhood, a strikingly handsome sandstone monolith rising in lone splendour above the plains.

From there on it is strictly a four-wheel drive track, and a very difficult one at that. There are more than ten kilometres of red sand dunes to be negotiated before arriving at the Pillar's base.

It is only 160 kilometres south of Alice Springs but this is tough, lonesome country. Chambers is a 50 metre sandstone pillar that towers over the landscape, a real monster of a solitary column lording it over a couple of lesser mounds and over thousands of hectares of nothingness.

Stuart, heading north on his earliest attempt to cross Australia, first saw it in April 1860 and it has remained a prominent landmark in Central Australia since then.

John Ross was the next European to visit

the area on 22 September 1870. Ross was returning from his journey to determine the route for the Overland Telegraph Line.

In 1872, the sound of hobble chains and European voices announced the arrival of another visitor, Ernest Giles (of Ayers Rock fame). He had come from the tiny settlement of Charlotte Waters on the newly completed Telegraph Line in his attempt to cross the continent to the west Australian coast.

This remarkable man of insatiable curiosity perhaps described the monument best. 'Clothed in white sandstone, mystic, wonderful,' he said.

It is that and more. The Pillar is above all a landmark of outstanding beauty. It stands without peer or challenge, a truly magnificent example of nature's many moods. In the evening it looks full of happiness, bursting with red, white and purple, dressed to go. But later, under the moon, its utter loneliness becomes transparent. It is a giant and helpless ghost sheeted in pale silver and forced to watch the passing of time. In the morning, however, the joy of the sun returns and with it another marvellous day.

Until the coming of the railway in the 1920s the Pillar was to be a landmark in the desert on the long overland journey from Adelaide to Alice Springs. Many of those early travellers have left their record in the soft, white sandstone.

Unfortunately so have some more recent visitors, clowns and vandals whose sole claim to glory are a few badly scratched syllables in the middle of nowhere. As a pamphlet by the Conservation Commission says, these early inscriptions, very often records of tenacity and hardship, now share less gracious company. Indeed.

But the Pillar would not be what it is, a fascinating landmark in Australian history, without the Aboriginal contribution. In the Aboriginal Dreamtime it is said the Gecko ancestor, Itirkawara, left the Finke River and journeyed northeastward. As he travelled he grew into a powerfully built man of superhuman strength and extreme violence of temper.

On the way home to his birthplace he successfully challenged and killed, with his stone knife, a number of other unfortunate ancestors. Flushed with the ease of his success he then disregarded the strict marriage code and took a wife from the wrong kin group.

His enraged relatives promptly banished him and the girl. The two retreated into the desert, Itirkawara raging in impotent fury, the girl shrinking from him in deep shame. Among the dunes they became weary and turned into prominent rocky formations— Itirkawara into the Pillar, the girl, still turning her face away from him in shame, into the low hill to the northeast, about 500 metres away.

As with other features in Centralia, the best time of the day to view the Pillar is at sunset and sunrise. The great column glows like a burning ember as the rays of the sun strike its face. For an overnight stay at the base of Chambers Pillar the Conservation Commission has provided barbecue fireplaces and tables for the use of visitors. Please ensure that fires are lit only in the appropriate receptacles.

We decided to return to Alice Springs on the Old South Road, a dirt track in fairly good condition. This track gave us a chance to see the Ewaninga Rock Carvings, not far from the Alice itself.

Ewaninga is only a small six hectare reserve but it provides immensely valuable links with the activities of early man in Australia. It consists of a claypan, a natural bowl for trapping and holding scarce rains, making this a favourite site for nomadic Aborigines who could rest for a while and hunt animals attracted to the water.

They had time and they used it to record their beliefs and history. It is not known exactly how old the carvings are but one thing is for certain, they predate present Aborigines in the area. The site therefore is of intense archaeological and anthropological value. It is important that the carvings are protected from unthinking vandals who may do to them what they have done to Chambers Pillar.

There are no camping facilities here

The free-standing cliffs of Rainbow Valley form part of the James Range. They are particularly attractive in the early morning and late afternoon, when the rainbow-like bands are highlighted.

PHOTOGRAPH BY FRANK WOERLE

PHOTOGRAPH BY DEREK ROFF

Ewaninga carvings. The early Aboriginal carvings at Ewaninga Conservation Reserve are a fragile remnant of a much earlier time. The designs on these outcrops of soft sandstone are very delicate and should be treated with care.

although wood barbecues, rustic picnic furniture and a pit toilet have been installed. Important to note is that there is no water either. If you venture here from Alice Springs, and I think the trip is well worthwhile, bring your own water.

Best time of the year to visit both the Pillar and Ewaninga is from March to October inclusive. It can get very hot in the summer months.

Also, on the way back to Alice Springs I suggest you stop over at the Rainbow Valley, not far south on the Stuart Highway. It is an enormously appealing valley formed by a delicate enclosure of tumbled cliffs. I confess to some disappointment when I arrived in the middle of the day. The valley looked undeserving of its name. There were

no colours except the usual red and pale ochre so often found in Central Australia and it was very hot, indeed uncomfortably so. Then evening came and the sun retired for the night. There was an absolute transformation here. The indifferent cliffs became Cinderella and dressed for a gala dance. I have never seen such a stunning change in such an incredibly short time. Now there was a semicircular gallery of broken cliffs bidding farewell and good riddance. Suddenly the scene changed to one of such exquisite beauty that it left me literally breathless.

Nothing quite prepares you for Rainbow Valley. No wonder it is such a sought after place by photographers and painters.

riodia spreads across the country by constantly growing outwards. As one of the outer branches bends downwards it takes root and starts a fresh plant.

PHOTOGRAPH BY STEVE STRIKE

184

DESERTS & SALTLAKES

No account of the wonders of the Northern Territory would be complete without at least a brief mention of the desert. The word itself has a very special mystique. It conjures up images of sun, sand, thirst and death.

The images are real enough. The Territory's two main deserts, the Simpson and Tanami, east and west of Alice Springs respectively, are just like that. There is a lot of sand, it can be extremely hot, and unless the travellers carry adequate water provisions and know what they are doing they may perish. Many have died and no doubt more will. Deserts are most unforgiving of fools and intolerant of mistakes.

The Simpson and Tanami do nevertheless provide unequalled experiences in terms of scenery, wild life and sheer adventure. For a start, they are vast, bigger than some European nations. They are also moody and surprising. After rains they sprout blankets of multicoloured flowers. As far as the eye

can see there is a kaleidoscope of purples and yellows, of reds and golds interspersed with greenery. The Simpson, especially, hides a peculiar kindness and gentility behind an austere facade. Its vast claypans full of water appear quite suddenly to a weary traveller that has just rounded the last sand dune. The water, warm on top, is usually cold at the bottom because sedimentary refuse on the surface will not allow the rays of the sun to pass through. Nothing like a cold bath at the end of a sweltering hot day in the sand.

But those two regions are fairly well known and need little explanation. Much less known and probably more interesting is the region between Tennant Creek/Warrego and Lajamanu (Hooker Creek), a 400 kilometre track in a region crying to be discovered.

The 60 kilometre road from Tennant Creek to the mining settlement at Warrego is sealed and well frequented. But the 400 kilometre four-wheel track from Warrego to

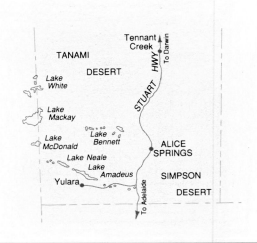

*The wide
expanse of
Lake Amadeus
defeated an 1872
exploration party
led by Giles, who
was attempting to
reach Ayers Rock.*

PHOTOGRAPH BY DEREK ROFF

187

esert grass (Triodia), a needle-like grass offering protection to small reptiles and mammals from large predators.

PHOTOGRAPH BY DEREK ROFF

Lajamanu does not appear in maps and is almost untravelled.

This is the track I decided to take in the company of David Fuller and a veteran ranger and superb bushman, Frank Woerle. Just a word of warning. Do not even attempt to travel this way after rains, even slight showers. If you are caught in the middle by a downpour just sit and wait. Even the sturdiest four-wheel drive vehicle will not get you out of the bog and there is a very good chance you may be forced to remain where you are until the weather dries or you are rescued.

That means you have to take plenty of water and food with you, enough for a week, just in case. Tell the police at Tennant Creek you are heading towards Lajamanu and when you get there report to the police as well. Preferably, have a radio in your vehicle.

Provided you follow those simple rules

you are in for a great experience. For nothing can be compared with the desert. Sure, you may spend a magnificent holiday on the palm-fringed beaches of Bali or go for a skiing trip to Thredbo. You may even learn to relax in the green, green fields of home or sit in front of a television set and enjoy your own peculiar Temple of Doom.

But in the desert you become another person. You are freer, cleaner, closer to the stars. And you are at one with extraordinary beauty.

It occurred to me as we made our way slowly to the northwest that I had seldom seen anything quite as haughty and majestic as this vast silent grandeur.

Here there was silence, barely a sigh from a gentle wind, just the hint of a contained whisper, a lover's murmur.

We camped at a rise, not much more than a slight ripple that nevertheless gave us a full circle of views. For me, the world came

$\mathcal{T}$he honey ant (Camponotus sp.) is a highly prized Aboriginal delicacy. The ants' underground nest, built in mulga woodland, is recognised by a series of small external holes under leaf litter. Up to 100 replete ants are found in small separate chambers in the nest. The stored honey is used to feed immature ants, or as reserves for times of food shortage.

PHOTOGRAPH BY DEREK ROFF

The spinifex hopping mouse, a nocturnal creature which feeds on grass seeds and small insects, is a favourite prey of feral cats.

PHOTOGRAPH BY DEREK ROFF

The thorny devil is an expert in camouflage and will vary its body colouring according to its environment.

PHOTOGRAPH BY D. CLARILE

The woma, or desert python, has a reputation for devouring other snake species—larger snakes are often noticeably restless in the presence of a woma.

PHOTOGRAPH BY BOB DARKEN

to a stop. Indeed I wished it so.

To the west was the most stunning sunset. To the east a storm blackened the horizon. The clouds in between were multihued, as if they could not make up their minds whether to go with the sun or with the rain. Below was the earth, smelling of wood and shrubs, of sand and rocks.

I sat transfixed watching the world around me. It was perfect.

Later, with the sky refusing to die, we lit a bright fire with gidgee wood—the wood of the desert that is so hard it can puncture a tough tyre—and grilled a few steaks which we washed down with cold beer.

After clearing a patch of spinifex, I put my sleeping-bag some distance from the embers and watched the stars.

Next morning we began the slow, long drive to Lajamanu through country with the rarest of vegetation and immensely courageous, tough little animals defying nature. The Aboriginal settlement, like any sign of human habitation, is a disappointment after that.

One wants the desert to go on and on—the tiny sandy hillocks, shrivelled plants and azure sky against yellow spinifex. There is a kind of purity, red and untainted, that no work of mortals can approach.

The road to Wave Hill from Lajamanu is reasonable. Wave Hill is well worth a visit because it is the place where the Aboriginal land rights movement started back in 1966/67 when the Gurindji walked off the Vestey station and camped at Wattie Creek demanding land they could call their own. The protest sent huge political waves across the country which culminated almost ten years later in the Land Rights (Northern Territory) Act of 1976.

There is a dirt track from Wave Hill to Victoria River Downs but the police advise against using it. The track has apparently not been used for some time and it may be impassable in parts. Although somewhat longer, the best advice is to follow the main road from Wave Hill to Top Springs and then turn westward towards Timber Creek.

Two places of interest on the way are the historical Victoria River Downs Station and Jasper Gorge which offers a good camping spot but no other facilities.

The Jasper Gorge features in some tourism pamphlets and glossy magazines as a unique example of geological architecture and beauty. Jasper Creek, which carved the gorge, was first crossed by the explorer Augustus Gregory in 1858 during his northern exploration journeys. It is well worth a stopover and provides a fitting farewell to the desert.

Shield shrimps appear in profusion after heavy rain but can lie dormant for many years when waterholes dry.

PHOTOGRAPH BY FRANK WOERLE

The galah feeds and roosts in noisy groups, and when airborne has a wild, erratic flight pattern that is easily recognisable.

URBAN PARKS & RESERVES

*F*inally, a brief mention of some Conservation Commission Parks and Reserves which, because they are so much taken for granted, perhaps escape attention.

They are the reserves and parks within the Northern Territory's urban centres or close to them. Locals and visitors often think of these parks merely as welcome amenities because that is precisely what they are. But they are also beautiful in their own right and well worth mentioning.

The following is by no means an exhaustive list, just of some of the more popular and familiar places.

Start with Darwin's Casuarina Coastal Reserve. It may surprise readers to know that more people come here than to Kakadu or Uluru. Visitors tend to be mainly locals who enjoy the opportunity to picnic, swim and fish on Darwin's doorstep.

The Casuarina Coastal reserve covers an area of 1180 hectares along the coast of Darwin's northern suburbs (where most Darwinians live), extending from Rapid Creek through to Lee Point.

There are some very interesting natural and historical features in the reserve. Beaches and dune systems give way to mangrove and monsoon vine thickets. On drier sites there are also patches of rainforest and paperbarks.

In historical terms, Old Man Rock is a registered Aboriginal sacred site. The Rock is in fact an outcrop of rocks that emerge from the sea on low tide directly opposite Dripstone Park. Fishing is permitted, but disturbing the rocks in any way or removing shellfish is prohibited.

And on the beach and cliffs are World War 2 artillery observation posts providing a graphic reminder of the area's wartime involvement (Darwin was the only Australian capital city to suffer from devastating Japanese aerial attacks.)

Wildlife abounds here. Sea and water dwelling creatures such as hermit crabs, snails and cockles are everywhere. Species of bats and bandicoots are also active at night foraging for food.

Spectacular birdlife such as ospreys, sea eagles, cormorants and gulls can be seen along the dunes or soaring overhead. And in the Wet the amazing little whimbrels come all the way from Siberia for their summer holiday. They often fraternise with other tourists, little greenshanks, from Asia.

As with the rest of the Top End coast, the Casuarina Beach has its share of dangerous creatures including the box jellyfish (sea wasps) and saltwater crocodiles. Box jellyfish are prevalent during the wet season months (October–May). The sting is extremely painful and can on occasions be fatal. If a sting occurs, the rangers recommend three steps: immobilise the victim, douse the affected area with vinegar, and seek medical help.

The huge central aviary at the Territory Wildlife Park is but one of its many attractions.

PHOTOGRAPH BY THE CONSERVATION COMMISSION

Saltwater crocodiles have been sighted in the Darwin harbour, Buffalo Creek and on all suburban beaches. These areas are regularly patrolled by rangers and crocs removed.

The reserve offers a good range of facilities for visitors. At Dripstone Park there are picnic areas with barbecues, park furniture, showers, toilets, children's playground and a kiosk.

There is also a free (nude) beach. Users who wish to bathe or suntan in the nude are required to stay within the signposted boundaries of the free beach although in Darwin's free and easy atmosphere, it really does not seem to matter very much.

For something different you may wish to drive about 65 kilometres southeast of Darwin to the Berry Springs Nature Park and Wildlife Park. I predict these two parks, often taken as one because they are only three kilometres away from each other, will become one of the Territory's foremost and best visited attractions in the near future.

The first reason for my prediction is that the area is very alluring in itself. Berry Creek, which flows through the park, is fed by a number of natural springs. The clear, rainforest fringed pools abound with small native fish and provide natural swimming areas for most of the year. This is a favourite for families on a Sunday outing.

Second is the superb Territory Wildlife Park which features much of the Territory's wildlife. Free-ranging exhibits are complemented by a spectacular underwater tunnel, a perfect vantage point to observe the aquatic life, a collection of bird aviaries in varying habitats and a splendid rainforest walk.

Of course if you are really interested in crocodiles, both freshies and salties, nothing can be compared with Darwin's crocodile farm which can be visited on the way to Berry Springs.

Finally, this park has good facilities for visitors. Parking, grassed picnic areas, barbecues, park furniture and toilets are

Ranger staff in the Territory's many parks and reserves can help to introduce you to the environment.

available. Firewood is supplied, so please do not take an axe to the surrounding bush.

For those interested in plants, the most attractive time to visit Berry Springs is the approach of the Dry (March–April) when many of the native plants are in flower and the vegetation is still green and luscious.

There is history here as well. Prior to the European settlement of the Top End, the Berry Springs area fell within the traditional homeland of the Larrakea tribe. It was used by Aboriginal people for hunting, camping and ceremonial purposes.

During World War 2, a rest and recreation camp was set up by the armed forces for the 100 000 personnel based in the area. A number of huts and a weir (similar to that found in another delightful recreational park near Darwin, Howard Springs) were built at Berry Springs. Their remains are still evident around the pool area. It speaks volumes for the regenerative powers of nature that years of this kind of treatment appear to have left no traces or done any

lasting harm to this charming area.

Further down the track to Katherine, a visit to the Low Level Nature Park should not be missed. It is a relatively small park, just 104 hectares, around the low level crossing on the Stuart Highway just outside the township.

The full width of the river valley for some three kilometres is included in the park and the greenery of the two steep banks provides a very pleasant backdrop to the picnic areas on the river's edge. During the dry season the lower areas are used by locals and visitors as a picnic and swimming site.

The water flows clean and shallow through the park throughout the Dry and is only a metre or so deep. In the Wet, however, a completely different picture emerges. Floods up to 18 metres above the dry season level flow through the full width of the valley. At this time the lower parking, picnic areas and toilets are often completely submerged for long periods. That is the

PHOTOGRAPH BY MIKE GILLAM

The protection of wildlife is aided by the establishment of our own parks and reserves.

nature of the Territory. Gentle and kind one day, fierce and scowling the next.

The flora here is quite varied. Common are the grey box, wide-leafed bloodwood, red-flowering kurrajong, wild kapok, bat-winged coral tree, paperbarks and fresh-water mangrove trees.

Barramundi, black and bony bream, rifle fish, alligator-jawed garfish and eel-tailed catfish are all found in the waters of the park. Fishing with hand line or rod and line only is permitted. Nets and spearguns are not.

Of course there are also freshwater crocodiles (but no salties here) and tortoises.

Wallabies, brush-tailed possums and more than 120 species of birds use the park as a refuge. For those interested in birdlife the rangers here have compiled a full checklist.

On to Alice Springs where it would be almost a sacrilege to miss a visit to the old Telegraph Station. Beautifully preserved and kept intact by the Conservation

Commission, the Telegraph Station provides one of the most striking examples of the lonely lives led by pioneering men and women who built and operated Australia's umbilical cord with the world.

The Station was midway along the Overland Telegraph Line from Darwin which played a key role in Australia's development.

Opened in 1872, the line suddenly reduced the isolation of Australians from their kith and kin on the other side of the globe. The exchange of personal and business messages now took hours instead of the months it previously took by sea.

This is living history on Alice Springs' doorstep and, icing on the cake, the scenery is breathtaking.

A 400 metre walk followed by a 30 metre rock scramble will get you on top of Trig Hill for better views of the Station.

From here Alice Springs is barely visible. In the distance is the striking moonscape of Central Australia. The Todd River,

The Alice Springs Telegraph Station has become an important educational facility for local school children with the introduction of the 'Alice on the Line' programme.

PHOTOGRAPH BY DEREK ROFF

Heavitree Gap, Tyuretya Hill, Mount Gillen, Simpsons Gap and Wallaby Gap all shine in the distance.

The Conservation Commission issues detailed guides and maps of the Telegraph Station. You will find that the restored buildings are very similar to the original and you can explore them by using a fold-out map. The map includes notes referring to places of interest. The rangers will help you if you would like to know more.

Incidentally, the Telegraph Line is connected with various places of historical interest along the Stuart Highway. For example, Ryan Well, hand dug by Paddy Ryan's team in 1889, is one of several wells sunk by the South Australian government along the track that followed the line. Drovers' sheep and cattle valued its salty water which was originally raised by a hand windlass.

In 1914, the Glen Maggie sheep and cattle station was established around this well and the owners charged a small fee per head to draw water for travelling stock.

The Glen Maggie homestead ruins are well preserved and a stark reminder of those hard, tough days.

Darwin's Botanic Gardens, now under the control of the Conservation Commission, provide a surprisingly compact and grand collection of the best flora the Top End can offer.

And there are now plans to improve on what has already been done, and indeed make the Gardens central to an ambitious project to convert Darwin into the best tropical city in the world.

Work has started on the vast project, which envisages linking the Botanic Gardens to Mindil Beach and the City proper.

These are just a few of the urban area parks the Conservation Commission manages in the Territory. Each has something to offer the visitor, whether a local resident or tourist. They are there for your enjoyment.

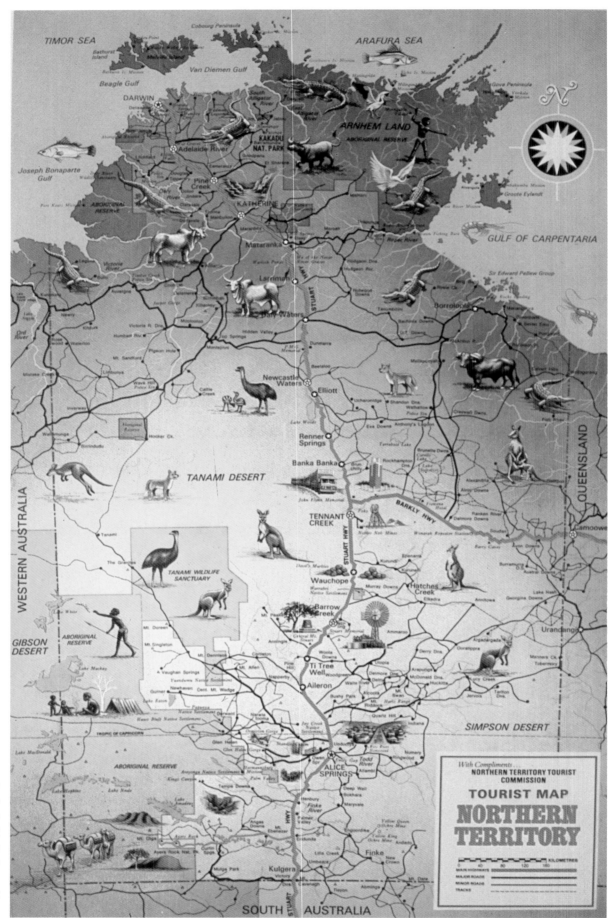

The map shows some of the more important historical sites which are accessible from the Stuart Highway.

PHOTOGRAPH BY CONSERVATION COMMISSION

198

THE STUART HIGHWAY

The Stuart Highway, known as the Track in the Northern Territory, is the umbilical cord that links the Northern Territory with the south and with the rest of Australia. It was so named to honour the persistence of John McDouall Stuart, who finally crossed the continent from south to north in 1861/62, at his fifth attempt.

For many visitors, the Stuart Highway is a long, monotonous, seemingly interminable stretch of bitumen between themselves and their destination. These travellers run the danger of missing the soul of the Territory, for the Track is more than just a road—its existence encapsulates this region's absurdly difficult history.

Its origins lie with the Overland Telegraph. This was a heroic undertaking, the result of an agreement between the South Australian colonial government and the British Australian Telegraph Company to establish electronic communications between Java, Port Darwin and Adelaide (and, subsequently, with the eastern seaboard of Australia).

The Overland Telegraph Line was completed on 23 August 1872. Beside it was a bush track built in fits and starts to enable wagons to bring supplies to the construction teams. It basically provided the outline for the future Stuart Highway.

One of the ways to examine the Stuart Highway is from the Overland Telegraph Stations dotted alongside it, which are carefully restored and maintained by the NT Conservation Commission. They provide a fascinating glimpse of the past, one that reveals the extraordinary vision and faith in the future of early Australians. They built the Overland Telegraph because they were confident in themselves and in their country.

Another way to appreciate this highway is by looking at its links with World War 2.

Until World War 2, the Track was indeed a bush track meandering among the Overland Telegraph poles. The dirt track was largely unused and Port Darwin remained a small and exotic frontier outpost.

As early as 1935, D. D. Smith, resident engineer with the Commonwealth Department of Works in Alice Springs, had proposed a five-year plan to the Department of Interior to build a road to modern standards between the Alice and Darwin. It was to replace the bush track alongside the Overland Telegraph.

After the ferocious Japanese bombing of Darwin on 19 February 1942, it was believed Northern Australia was about to be invaded, so major military development occurred. The build-up would not have been possible without an all-weather north–south road.

The enduring myth is that the Americans built the Stuart Highway. This is not true. As I describe in another book, *Australia's Frontline: The Northern Territory's War*, the engineering feat was almost purely an Australian undertaking.

In July 1940, Colonel Murdock, Director General of Engineering Services, held a conference in Melbourne over the need to rush a military road between the two Territory centres. The first requisition was for a trafficable road designed to carry 220 tonnes per day each way. The problem was how to build it. The proposal was considered a major engineering work well beyond the capabilities of the Commonwealth's Department of Works or the military.

It was finally resolved that New South Wales, Queensland and South Australia would participate in a rare example of interstate cooperation. The arrangement was that South Australia should build the southern section from Tennant Creek to Ferguson Spring (199.6 kilometres);

Queensland on to Dunmara (145.6 kilometres); and New South Wales the northern section to Birdum (139.2 kilometres), the railhead of the Northern Australian Railway (also built late in the nineteenth century).

The construction of the modern Stuart Highway is a story of cooperation and achievement. South Australia, in 14 special trains, railed its crew and plant to Alice Springs, then drove the whole outfit to its base at Banka Banka.

Queensland railed its team to Mt Isa then, in a record convoy of massed machines and men, overlanded them 1046 kilometres to its main base at Newcastle Waters.

New South Wales sent its contribution by sea from Sydney to Darwin initially on the SS *Zealandia* on 3 September 1940, then by rail to Larrimah, about 500 kilometres south of Darwin. This outfit completed its task first, in just 63 days, almost immediately followed by Queensland and South Australia.

On 29 November 1940, Tennant Creek and the Larrimah railway siding were joined by a speedy traffic road 484.4 kilometres long. In March 1941, the Minister for the Army also approved the building of a road link from Mt Isa across the Barkly Tableland to join the north–south road 25 kilometres north of Tennant Creek. This road, continuously upgraded until 1944, became the Barkly Highway.

But no one anticipated the demands that the war would place upon the newly built highway. The original specification of 220 tonnes per day increased to 2700 tonnes soon after the war began. Indicative of the massive transport effort required was that the Darwin Overland Maintenance Force (DOMF) was originally made up of only 730 officers and men equipped with 150 three-tonne trucks. A relatively short time later, the DOMF was expanded to 8000 personnel and 3000 vehicles.

Then, during the big Wet of 1941/42 (November to March), five weeks of torrential rain broke down long stretches of the road surface and caused up to 100 vehicles at a time to bog down. Lieutenant Colonel Noel Loutit, the DOMF commander, inspected the road in March 1942 and reported it to be 'in the worst condition it has been in for the last 18 months'.

Six months later, General MacArthur's chief engineer, Brigadier General Hugh Casey, endorsed Loutit's view. It was the beginning of American involvement in the construction of the Stuart Highway, which started with the arrival of two modern Barber-Green plant mix units from the United States in 1942, and finished with the sealing of both highways by the end of 1944.

Almost all the work was done by more than 3000 Australians in the Civil Construction Corps, a compulsory service body to carry out projects for the Allied Works Council. Australians 'cleared, formed up, black-topped and maintained 954 miles between Darwin and Alice Springs'. The same applies to the stretch of the Stuart Highway between Darwin and Adelaide River, which was built in its entirety by the NSW Department of Main Roads. There was, however, a substantial contribution of equipment from the Americans.

The Track offers a chance to put yourself in the shoes of the airmen and soldiers who served in these remote wastes and endured enemy attacks, boredom, loneliness and danger until demobbed and sent back south.

Start at Alice Springs, itself a substantial military base during the war, and move north to the staging camp of Barrow Creek, located almost 30 kilometres north of Barrow Creek. The camp was operated mainly by the 5 Australian Personnel Staging Camp from 30 May 1942 until 28 February 1945. These were the indispensable logistics people who ensured that servicemen posted north were identified, clothed, fed and otherwise victualled. This site is considered one of the most significant in the Territory, because it was used by every person who travelled north by convoy.

I wonder if the soldiers were even aware they had established their base near the site of one of the many bloody encounters

between Aboriginals and white settlers in the Territory. On 22 February 1874, a group of Aborigines from the Gaididja tribe attacked the staff of the Barrow Creek telegraph station and killed the station master, J. Stapleton, and one J. Franks, before being repelled by intense fire from other staff.

A punitive expedition was immediately ordered out under Trooper Samuel Gason, who rode around the countryside for some two months killing as many Aborigines as he found. No one knows the exact number of blacks shot to death, but as many as 50 could have been killed.

Move next to Elliott, a place originally named No 8 Bore Newcastle Waters. This became a classic example of a township built by the military as early as 1940 and occupied by the Darwin Overland Maintenance Force. Named after Army Lieutenant 'Snow' Elliott, who established No 7 Australian Personnel Staging Camp in the area, the new township had three officers and 81 'other ranks'. Elliott eventually acquired the capacity to shelter 1500 men and boasted a vegetable garden kept evergreen with bore water.

Other small centres up the Track that experienced enormous dislocation through the armed build-up were Larrimah, Birdum, and Banka Banka. Birdum was of particular importance because of its strategic role. The northern campaign, which stretched from Darwin and the airfields just south all the way to the Netherlands East Indies (Indonesia), was run from the pub.

Road visitors to the Top End can see the remnants of the railway line from Birdum to Darwin. It went out of existence in 1976, but the NAR line in fact played a crucial role during the war years. Affectionately known as Leaping Lena, it carried thousands of troops and tonnes of supplies from about 1942 to 1945.

The impact of the wartime influx of Americans on the tiny settlement of Birdum was considerable. The handful of locals, hardy Territorians unaccustomed to strangers, were suddenly swamped by people. During those heady days, Birdum boasted of a hotel and outhouses and a well-patronised war theatre. The settlement reverted to a sleepy hollow immediately after the war.

Not far away was the huge airfield of Gorrie, built between 1942 and 1943 just north of Larrimah and named after Flight Officer P. Gorrie, who was killed on a mission over Menado with No 2 Squadron on 1 January 1942. There were 90 Comet or Sidney Williams huts, 4 Bellman and 6 Singapore hangars. There was also a depot cinema, and, when conditions had become less dangerous, an Airmen's Recreation Hall for mixed dancing.

Another base was established at Mataranka Station Homestead, some 10 kilometres south of the township. Stirling Mill, 14 kilometres north of Mataranka township, was the site of an airforce sawmill originally operated by No 1 Flight Engineering Construction Section of the RAAF.

Of course, Mataranka itself became a major base with 9 headquarter units, 2 Provosts, 7 Engineer, 5 AEME, 23 Ordnance, 14 Supply and Transport, 1 Infantry, 3 Postal, 4 Intelligence, 9 Medical, 10 Miscellaneous, 1 Pay and 13 Signals.

Katherine, which was bombed once during the war, also boasted two airfields, at Manbullo Station and at Tindal. The latter is now a major RAAF base and the nearby Delamere Station is a state-of-the-art air-to-ground bombing range. Katherine also was the training site of Independent Company's Commandoes, who were sent to Timor. This was the only Allied unit in South-East Asia never to surrender to the enemy.

Adelaide River, where civilians and military personnel fleeing the devastating Japanese raids on Darwin congregated, was the first small settlement to experience change. Already a very substantial military base, it experienced a huge build-up after February 1942. It is now the home of an official war cemetery.

The road between Adelaide River and Darwin is dotted with the sites of old airfields and military bases from which an all-out effort was made against the Japanese in the huge Indonesian archipelago. But for General Douglas MacArthur's decision to carry the main thrust of the war in the Pacific (the so-called island hopping campaign) this would have been the staging base for the final assault on Japan. As it was, the Northern Territory was the launching pad for the longest bombing flights in World War 2.

The Stuart Highway is more than just a road. It is an engineering and historical land-mark, one well worth examining for its own value, not just as a relatively comfortable link between south and north.

The 4-WD track takes you to Arltunga first. This is the scene of one of the last gold rushes in Australia in the late 19th century. They came from all over the country with their horses and mules or pushing wheelbarrows, tough men prepared to defy the Centralian harshness for an elusive dream of wealth.

PHOTOGRAPH BY CONSERVATION COMMISSION

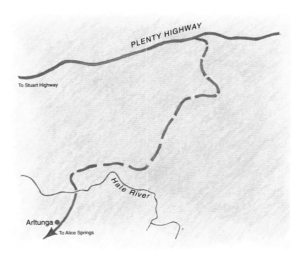

'TERRITORY EXPLORER'

Now travellers who may be somewhat jaded have the opportunity to embark on a new adventure in the Territory. Be warned. It is not for everybody, nor will it attract the faint-hearted. If you go, you will enter a new world, one of great challenges and exuberant freedoms, where you will step into the past, sometimes the very remote past, and may emerge a different person.

This is where the 'Territory Explorer' will lead you. It is a long four-wheel drive track that will eventually link Central Australia with the Top End of the Territory, then stretch out to north-western Australia. The track is tough and demanding and winds through some of the most remote corners of Outback Territory. Here, you are alone. It is just you and the country—forbidding, hard but ultimately, generous and infinitely beautiful.

'Territory Explorer' does exactly what it says, it explores the Northern Territory in ways that more formal tours to more sedate and well-trodden destinations can never do.

Before I describe three relatively short links of the 'Territory Explorer' as examples, a few things should be mentioned. One is that the track must be approached with caution. You will be driving a vehicle in top condition into some of the most inhospitable and unforgiving terrain in the world. As with the rest of the Territory, the land seems deceptively gentle. But it is extraordinarily cruel with people who do not take reasonable precautions.

Also note, before you embark on this truly remarkable adventure, you should notify Conservation Commission rangers or the police about your route and estimated time of arrival wherever you are going.

Let us start with what I have named the Gem Route. It runs from Arltunga, east of Alice Springs, to the Plenty Highway to the north, a distance of about 90 kilometres. North of the highway you enter the Dulcie Range, but that is another story. The Gem Route does two things. It allows you a taste of Outback Central Australia and a toss of the dice at fossicking.

The track runs over broken and spectacular terrain, it weaves and winds from surprise to surprise. Suddenly, you find yourself in the sands of a small waterhole, at the foot of an angry cliff, next you are in the midst of a stunted and gnarled forest that will not let you look beyond the immediate environs.

This country demands respect. This is a passionate and erratic area, one that will keep you guessing and wondering. Just when you think the worst may be over, it begins again. Down to a dry creek bed and up those seemingly arrogant rocky hills that will not accept domination. With no warning, quite abruptly, you are in one of the oases that the country offers as a gift.

Here you will find wild passionfruit (sometimes known as capers) along dried watercourses, with their roots deep in heavy clay so that they can survive without rain. There are also red-bud mallees, related to the eucalypt, which give out a red pod that breaks into a myriad gold tendrils to greet the sun. Occasionally, you see rush-leaf grevillea with brilliant flowers that birds love because of their honey-like nectar. And there are blue mallees, curry wattles and holly grevilleas with bright red grape-like bunches.

With some luck, you may catch sight of a grey shrike thrush singing its melodious call, or a peregrine falcon searching for a flock of green budgerigars. There are also goannas and wallabies and big euros around as well as the odd emu and bustard.

The track is interesting for another reason. It takes you to the best fossicking fields in Central Australia. Zircon, garnets, ionites and other precious stones are found here in relative abundance. About 5000 fossickers from all over the world come to this region annually to try their luck, and they have a lot of fun doing it.

If, when you visited Arltunga, you wondered about the world of prospectors and miners in years gone by, here you have a chance to live in that world. Visitors who do not fancy the roughness of the four-wheel drive track from the old mining settlement can approach the gem field via the Plenty Highway. There are several operators in the area who rent out equipment. In the likely event that you find something, one of the operators, Gemtree, will cut your stones and post them home for you.

This is an immensely enjoyable span, which combines direct contact with the best nature has to offer in Central Australia, with just that touch of adventure and risk.

The second span will take you deep into the Great Central Desert in the Tanami Region. You will need a permit from the Central Land Council for this part of your trip, because you are entering Aboriginal land.

Some of this region has been described elsewhere in the book, but what made my September 1993 trip so startlingly different was the recent tumultuous rains, which created two vast freshwater lakes teeming with life. This was the inland ocean that pioneering explorers looked for and did not find. The rains also washed out the existing track, making progress hazardous and slow. But what a magnificent experience it was to see the marvellously delicate flowers and incredible shrubs come alive in the red sand. The sturdy desert oaks were no longer alone, but had all these little friends to share their splendid space. And where before only a few lizards and small snakes gathered the courage to venture into this immense loneliness, now birds of all kinds and even a few clumsy camels and wallabies could be found. Once, I saw the footprints of a huge dingo but did not catch sight of the animal.

There were shrimp in the lakes, full of joy at the miracle that had brought life to eggs which had been buried for years. They would not live for too long, probably no more than two or three months, when the inland seas will vanish. In that time, they would mate and procreate and, in turn, their tiny fertile eggs would disappear back into the sand. Some will survive. Burrowed deep into their cosy sand cocoons, they will wait maybe for many years until torrential rains come once more and the cycle will start again.

It is the same with plants, those hugely fragile and appealing flowers that are not at all similar to relatives in more temperate climates or environments. Here, they appear only when conditions are propitious, perhaps once every five or ten years, and they grace the land with such charm that one wants them to grow for ever. There was a blanket of stunted grevilleas with yellow fruit attracting birds of all kinds to its honey. The ground was a sea of incredibly delicate plants, which bloomed tiny specks of blue, yellow and red.

But they, too, like the shrimp and the little fish, disappear and the landscape returns to its harsh and angry red mask, disguising its gentle heart. The wallabies, the camels, the dingoes — they all leave. It is then easy to forget that this place is paradise after the rains.

It can also be hell for the unwary. Do not forget. If you want to, here you can find yourself, because nowhere else offers the same overwhelming sense of seclusion. The desert is the ultimate retreat. But it can kill unless you take some fairly commonsense

This is what remains of the gold miner's dreams, a few stone cottages at Arltunga now restored by the Conservation Commission. They have not yet been claimed by the desert and stand as mute testimony to their pioneering effort.

steps. Find out what those are with the nearest NT Conservation Commission station and then set off for an unforgettable journey.

The track will take you to Lajamanu (Hooker Creek) on the northern fringe of the Great Central Desert. North again from Lajamanu stretches a good gravel road that will take you to the Buchanan Highway, built along a stock route and named after the pioneering cattleman. You come to a place called Kalkaringi, halfway between Wave Hill on the north-east and Daguragu on the south-east. Kalkaringi, like Wave Hill and Daguragu, may look like just a collection of cottages under the boiling sun. But if that is all you see you are missing one of the most important watersheds in Australian history, for this small triangle of land is the cradle of land rights and, indeed, of the Aboriginal Movement across the country. It is also the heart of the Northern Territory's Victoria River District and therefore the quintessential companion of the great frontier cattle culture.

Here, pioneering cattlemen clashed with some of the most warlike Aboriginal tribes in the continent. Boomerangs and spears were no match for Martini Henrys and Winchesters, and the tribes, one by one, were eventually subjugated or killed.

While you camp out near a billabong you may want to read *Hidden Stories* by Deborah Bird Rose, an exceedingly good account of this area's rich history. But Ernestine Hill's *The Territory* perhaps explains the story best. She says, among other things:

The business of establishing a cattle empire depended upon killing. To the new station you brought working blacks from some far country—no conspiracies, they were terrified of the 'bush niggers', and for protection of your 'muckity', musket, never ventured out of your sight. There was 'quiet nigger' country and 'bad nigger' country ...

As Bird Rose says, 'The Victoria River Valley was, from the point of view of the settlers, most assuredly, "bad nigger country".'

The cattle barons established their empires, and around them grew a whole industry of cattleduffers or poddy dodgers, who were in fact welcomed by the cattlemen, mainly because the ruffians came at a price well worth paying. They were the

buffer between the established cattle stations and the Aboriginals in the surrounding bush.

Typical of the cattleduffers was Brigalow Bill, who took up a block on the west side of Victoria River around 1908. His notorious career ended in 1910, when he was ambushed and killed by a group of Aborigines. Nor was the killing confined to white versus black. Early this century, the great intertribal wars over women also took a dreadful toll of the Aboriginal population in the area, as did smallpox epidemics.

In 1967, however, Aborigines here began a long fight back, which eventually led to land rights and to a degree of self-determination. In that year, a group led by Vince Lingiari struck for higher pay at Wave Hill. When the rise was not granted, they adjourned to nearby Wattie Creek to sit out the strike. This simple industrial dispute escalated into demands for land, first a small block of about 7 square kilometres around Wattie Creek, then into land rights.

Take in all of this before you move on to the best-kept secret in the Top End, the 75 kilometre track from Sanford Station north to Humbert River Station. To get to Sanford Station, you follow a well-graded and well-kept track from Daguragu almost straight north to the station.

Sanford is a showpiece of the Territory's cattle industry. It is a great pastoral station, immaculately kept, where the rolling hills and tidy paddocks will remind visitors of stations in Victoria or South Australia.

As you cross the last gate before Humbert River on the station's northern boundary,

you move into another world. This is one of the most scenic parts of the Top End and hardly anyone visits it. The very rough four-wheel drive track winds among well-forested hills and magnificent escarpments for about 40 kilometres, crisscrossed by many waterways which were dry in September, but which are impassable in the Wet.

And now you come upon one of those places which, for no reason that you can explain, evokes or rekindles something that has perhaps lain inert in your spirit and you did not even know was there.

This is the Gibbie Gorge. I have not been able to find another name for it (although some Conservation Commission rangers appear to believe it should be called the Wickham Gorge, as the Gibbie is a tributary of the Wickham River) because it does not feature in maps, but since it is between the Gibbie Creek and an astonishingly beautiful escarpment, the name seems to fit.

There are other escarpments and creeks in the Top End. What makes this one exceptional is an immensely dark primeval forest that stretches for about 10 kilometres at the bottom of the unnamed escarpment. Here is a jumbled mess of northern box and bloodwood, fine tall eucalypt, whitewood and beefwood, with vines hanging lazily to clean ground mulched by millions of years of refuse and decay. It is an inviting forest with a mysterious depth that you may want to enter and explore. There is infinite peace here in this remote corner, waiting to be discovered.

Finally, the third lap, which runs along

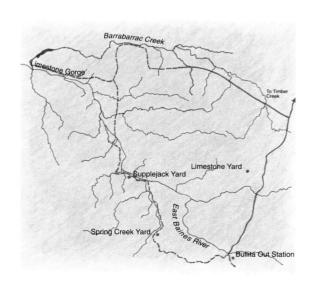

A tributary of the East Baines River about 51 kilometres north of Bullita Station. This was a drovers' rest campsite and is now an inviting camping spot for 4-WD enthusiasts willing to venture into Gregory Park.

PHOTOGRAPH BY CONSERVATION COMMISSION

the Bullita stock route in the Gregory National Park, near Timber Creek. This is an old droving route, which will take you into the remote western section of the Park. The route originally led all the way to Wyndham in north-western Australia. A very tough route opened up by very tough men.

To get there, follow a four-wheel drive track north from Humbert River Station to the Park itself. It is well marked with star pickets and winds over picturesque but rough country all the way to the old Durack Bullita homestead described elsewhere in the book.

The specially constructed four-wheel drive challenge runs over 92 kilometres and is divided into eight stops. You won't want to do it in one day, though it is possible.

The temptations along the route are irresistible.

Let me tell you of just three of those. The first takes you to Spring Creek Jump Up, an unusually beautiful series of water ponds among tall limestone hills and tower karsts. The water here is limpid and inviting. It is an ideal spot for camping and forgetting the bone-jarring, gut-wrenching, eye-popping, teeth-rattling journey.

Nutwood and boabs rest amidst other typical Top End shrubbery. Nutwoods are better known as crocodile trees for their rough-textured, chequered bark that is similar in appearance to the back skin of a crocodile. Some pandanus fringe the clear pools below, in which the sunlight plays iridescent games. There is contentment in this place and maybe we

The 4-WD track ends at Bullita Station near Timber Creek in the Top End. The grandeur of the Gregory Park north of Humbert River unfolds before your eyes. This is the scenery that greeted pioneering cattlemen like the Duracks when they broke through to this country.

PHOTOGRAPH BY CONSERVATION COMMISSION

ask for too much when we ask for more.

The second spot is about 21 kilometres from the start, at the junction of Spring Creek and East Baines (named by explorer Augustus Gregory after the artist Thomas Baines, who discovered it on the North Australian expedition in 1855/56). A very large boab marks a droving camp site. Boabs were traditional meeting places and camp sites during droving and mustering. One of the boabs was inscribed 'Oriental Hotel', suggesting it was a regular camp site. Similar inscriptions, 'Club Hotel' and 'Royal Hotel', can be found along the Baines.

Here you can reflect on the life of those drovers. A typical droving team consisted of five or six men—a head stockman, cook, horse tailer and three or so others. The camps were disbanded at first light. Food consisted almost entirely of beef with potatoes and onions. Tea, flour and sugar were the only other food carried. Conservation Commission rangers would add coffee to that. Otherwise, they would reflect, life has not changed much.

The third camping spot I want to mention is about 51 kilometres from the start, at Drovers Rest Campsite, situated on the Barrabarrac Creek about 200 metres from the junction with East Baines River. Here you can fish for barramundi to your heart's content. But if grilled barra over red-hot

coals as the sun sets does not altogether please you, there are also archer fish. Called 'archer' because of their unusual hunting method, these fish capture insects on or above the water by shooting them with an accurately placed jet of water.

There is a 3 kilometre long waterhole on the East Baines itself, which is reached through the Barrabarrac Creek. Below the camp site, there is a natural boat ramp. Bushwalkers can find their way from here to the escarpments on the north-east, where some mysterious craters with unusual vegetation are found.

The meeting of Barrabarrac Creek and the East Baines River marks the convergence of the Auvergne Stock Route with the Bullita Stock Route. It was an important camp site and was commonly known by cattlemen as Drovers Rest. The Victoria River nearby is fed by eight such tributaries and is the longest river system in Australia.

There are only freshwater crocodiles where the Barrabarrac and East Baines meet, perhaps a welcome departure from the Victoria, where very large saltwater crocs abound.

After completing the exhilarating four-wheel drive trip, you will probably want a place where you can wash clothes and let someone else do the cooking for a change. It is only a short distance from the Bullita

Stock Route to Timber Creek on the Victoria Highway. There are good facilities at Timber Creek and the atmosphere is of a classic Top End small town, particularly during the annual race meeting early in September, when stockmen from the surrounding stations descend into the place for their yearly vacation.

Well, I hope you enjoy yourself. It is a once-in-a-lifetime experience, and probably the best way to explore Outback Australia.

APPENDIX: PARK FACILITIES

Facilities available to the public vary from park to park.
The following is a brief run down of what is available in the various parks, opening times (24 hours unless indicated) and whether four wheel drive is necessary or recommended.

GURIG NATIONAL PARK

Four wheel drive is necessary and a permit is required from the Conservation Commission.

Picnic facilities are available, camping is allowed, guided tours are available, fishing is allowed and a boat ramp is available. Drinking water is available on site.

The road is not accessible when wet, there are no constructed walking tracks and no toilets for the handicapped.

WILDMAN RIVER RESERVE

Camping and fishing are allowed.

There are no entry requirements and there are picnic facilities at Shady Camp, constructed walking tracks, guided tours, boat ramp, toilets for the handicapped or drinking water on site.

The road is not accessible when wet.

KAKADU NATIONAL PARK

The park is managed by the Australian National Parks and Wildlife Service and an entrance fee is applicable.

All other facilities are available including picnic facilities, walking tracks, camping, guided tours, fishing, boat ramp, toilets for the handicapped and drinking water.

The road is accessible all year round.

LITCHFIELD PARK

Camping is allowed and there are picnic facilities at Wangi Falls. Walking Tracks are under construction. There are toilets for the handicapped and drinking water on site.

There are no entry requirements, no guided tours available and the road is not accessible when wet. There is no fishing or boat ramp. Four wheel drive is highly recommended.

DALY RIVER NATURE PARK

Camping and fishing are allowed and there are picnic facilities and drinking water on site.

There are no entry requirements, no constructed walking tracks, no guided tours available, no boat ramp and no toilets for the handicapped.

The road is inaccessible when wet.

DOUGLAS HOT SPRINGS NATURE PARK

Camping and fishing are allowed and there are picnic facilities, walking tracks and drinking water on site.

There are no entry requirements, no guided tours, no boat ramp and no toilets for the disabled.

BUTTERFLY GORGE NATIONAL PARK

Camping and fishing are allowed and there are walking tracks and drinking water on site.

There are no entry requirements, no picnic facilities, no guided tours, no boat ramp and no toilets for the handicapped.

The road is inaccessible when wet.

WATERFALL CREEK NATURE PARK

An entrance fee is payable and camping and fishing are allowed. There are picnic facilities and drinking water on site.

There are no walking tracks, guided tours, boat ramps or toilets for the handicapped.

The road is inaccessible when wet.

UMBRAWARRA GORGE
NATIONAL PARK

Camping is allowed and there are picnic facilities and walking tracks.

There are no entry requirements, no guided tours, no fishing, boat ramps or drinking water.

The road is inaccessible when wet.

EDITH FALLS (KATHERINE GORGE NATIONAL PARK)

Camping and fishing are allowed and there are picnic facilities, walking tracks and drinking water.

There are no entry requirements, guided tours, boat ramps or toilets for the disabled.

The road is accessible when wet.

KATHERINE GORGE (NITMILUK NATIONAL PARK)

The park is open from 7 a.m. - 7 p.m. excluding the camping area.

There are no entry requirements, camping and fishing are allowed and facilities include picnic areas, walking tracks, guided tours, boat ramps, toilets for the disabled and drinking water on site.

The road is accessible when wet.

CUTTA CUTTA CAVES NATURE PARK

Open from 9 a.m. - 4.30 p.m. and a cave tour ticket can be obtained at the park before the tour starts.

There are picnic facilities, walking tracks, guided tours and drinking water available on site.

There is no camping, fishing, boat ramp or toilets for the disabled.

The road is accessible when wet.

MATARANKA THERMAL POOL NATURE PARK

Walking tracks are available and there are toilets for the disabled and drinking water on site.

Accommodation is available outside the park.

There are no entry requirements, picnic facilities, guided tours, fishing or boat ramps.

The road is accessible when wet.

KATHERINE LOW LEVEL NATURE PARK

Open from 7 a.m. - 7 p.m. and has picnic facilities, fishing, toilets for the disabled and drinking water on site.

There are no entry requirements, walking tracks, camping facilities or boat ramp.

The road is accessible when wet.

GREGORY NATIONAL PARK

Camping and fishing are allowed and there are ample picnic facilities, walking tracks, boat ramp and toilets for the disabled.

There are no entry requirements and no guided tours.

The road is accessible when wet.

KEEP RIVER NATIONAL PARK

Camping and fishing are allowed and there are picnic facilities, walking tracks and drinking water on site.

There are no entry requirements, guided tours or a boat ramp. The road is accessible when wet.

DEVILS MARBLES CONSERVATION RESERVE

Camping is allowed and there are picnic facilities and walking tracks.

There are no entry requirements, toilets for the disabled, or drinking water on site.

The road is accessible when wet.

TREPHINA GORGE NATURE PARK

Camping is allowed and there are picnic facilities, walking tracks, toilets for the disabled and drinking water on site.

There are no entry requirements or guided tours. The road is inaccessible when wet.

RUBY GAP NATURE PARK

Camping is allowed and picnic facilities are available. There are no entry requirements, walking tracks, guided tours, toilets for the disabled or drinking water.

The road is inaccessible when wet.

REDBANK NATURE PARK

Camping is allowed but there are no other facilities. There are no entry requirements and the road is inaccessible when wet.

ARLTUNGA HISTORICAL RESERVE

Accommodation is available outside the reserve and inside there are picnic facilities, walking tracks and toilets for the disabled.

There are no entry requirements or guided tours. The road is accessible when wet.

CHAMBERS PILLAR HISTORICAL RESERVE

Four wheel drive is necessary. Camping is allowed and there are picnic facilities.

There are no entry requirements, walking tracks, guided tours, toilets for the disabled or drinking water. The road is inaccessible when wet.

SIMPSONS GAP NATIONAL PARK

Open from 8 a.m. - 8 p.m. Picnic facilities, walking tracks, toilets for the disabled and drinking water are available.

There are no entry requirements, camping or guided tours. The road is inaccessible when wet.

STANDLEY CHASM

Open 8.30 a.m. - 4.30 p.m. Managed by the Iwupataka Aboriginal community.

Picnic facilities, walking tracks and drinking water are available.

There is a park entrance fee. Camping is not permitted, guided tours and toilets for the disabled are not available.

The road is accessible when wet.

SERPENTINE GORGE NATURE PARK

Camping is allowed and picnic facilities are available.

There are no entry requirements, walking tracks or guided tours. Drinking water and toilets for the disabled are not available.

The road is inaccessible when wet.

ORMISTON GORGE AND POUND NATIONAL PARK

Camping is allowed and picnic facilities are provided and there are toilets for the disabled and drinking water on site.

There are no guided tours and the road is accessible when wet.

GLEN HELEN GORGE NATURE PARK

Picnic facilities are provided and accommodation is available outside the park. Drinking water is available on site.

There are no entry requirements, walking tracks or guided tours.

The road is inaccessible when wet.

FINKE GORGE NATIONAL PARK

Four wheel drive is necessary, picnic facilities are provided and camping is allowed. There are toilets for the disabled and drinking water on site.

The road is inaccessible when wet.

HENBURY METEORITES CONSERVATION RESERVE

Picnic facilities are provided and camping is allowed.

There are no entry requirements, walking tracks, guided tours, toilets for the disabled or drinking water.

The road is accessible when wet.

KINGS CANYON NATIONAL PARK (WATARRKA)

Camping is allowed and there are picnic facilities and walking tracks as well as toilets for the disabled and drinking water.

There are no entry requirements or guided tours. The road is inaccessible when wet.

ULURU NATIONAL PARK

The park is managed by the Australian National Parks and Wildlife Service and there is an entry fee.

There are picnic facilities, walking tracks, guidetours, toilets for the handicapped and drinking water on site.

Accommodation is available outside the park. The road is inaccessible when wet.

212

INDEX